THE BATTLE OF ULUNDI

Lord William Beresford's encounter with a Zulu in the reconnaissance across the White Mfolozi, 3 July 1879. (*Illustrated London News,* 6 September 1879.)

The battle of Ulundi

JOHN LABAND

Cartography by
Helena Margeot
and
Raymond Poonsamy

Shuter & Shooter

KwaZulu Monuments Council

Other titles in this series:
King Cetshwayo kaMpande
by J. Laband and J. Wright
Fight us in the open
by J. Laband

Co-published by

Shuter & Shooter (Pty) Ltd
Gray's Inn, 230 Church Street
Pietermaritzburg, South Africa 3201

and

KwaZulu Monuments Council
Department of Education and Culture
Private Bag X04
Ulundi
3838

Copyright © KwaZulu Monuments Council

All rights reserved. No part of this publication may be reproduced or transmitted, in any form or by any means, without permission of the publishers

First edition 1988

ISBN 0 7960 0118 9

Set in 11 on 13 pt Baskerville
Printed by The Natal Witness (Pty) Ltd, Pietermaritzburg
5688L

In memory of

Frank Emery

Contents

Acknowlegements .... (viii)

Note on the location of amakhanda .... (x)

Note on the maps .... (x)

The British Army at the Battle of Ulundi .... (xi)

The Zulu Army at the Battle of Ulundi .... (xiv)

1 Warding off the British 1

2 At the White Mfolozi 10

3 Forming up in the plain 21

4 The battle 28

5 Assessing the cost 43

   Chronology 49

   Glossary 50

   References 52

Acknowledgments

I thank the Human Sciences Research Council and the University of Natal whose financial assistance in 1984 facilitated my research in England towards this little book. A number of people read it while in manuscript, and their comments, suggestions and corrections were much appreciated. I record my thanks to Tim Maggs, Val Ward, David Owen and, in particular, Mary Monteith of Shuter & Shooter, whose judgement I have learned to value most highly. Ian Knight's help with the illustrations was most welcome. Any shortcomings in the final product must remain my own, as are the opinions expressed and conclusions reached.

In addition, I am most grateful for the hospitality extended me while researching by Jonathan and Jane Ruffer, then of London; the late Frank Emery of St Peter's College, Oxford; David and Patricia Owen, then of Melmoth; and Jeremy and Gail Andrew of Johannesburg.

LIST OF MAPS

Map 1 — The British advance on the White Mfolozi
    from the Mthonjaneni heights 12
Map 2 — The British reconnaissance of 3 July 1879 17
Map 3 — The British square at the Battle of Ulundi 22
Map 4 — The Battle of Ulundi, 4 July 1879 30

Note on the location of amakhanda

Considerable archaeological work in the field is still required to confirm nineteenth-century descriptions and surviving oral tradition concerning the precise location of many *amakhanda*. Even when a site is known, its name can remain uncertain. Nevertheless, it has been possible to position and name many of the *amakhanda* mentioned in this book, and to depict them on maps. This would not have been possible without the knowledge and help of the following:

Prince Muntompofu kaMahlathini kaShingane Zulu
Mr J.K. Dladla, Organizer of Cultural Affairs, KwaZulu Department of
    Education and Culture, Ulundi.
Mr R. Rawlinson, Archaeology Research Unit, University of Zululand
Mr D. Owen, Historian of the KwaZulu Monuments Council, oNdini
Mr J. Nxumalo, retired schoolteacher and custodian at emGungundlovu

Note on the maps

Modern features which did not exist at the time of the battle of Ulundi, such as roads, railways, the modern town of Ulundi and the Legislative Assembly, have been depicted in light grey. The purpose of their inclusion is to assist today's visitors to the area in identifying the sites of 1879.

The British Army at the Battle of Ulundi

RECRUITMENT AND RANKS OF REGULAR BRITISH TROOPS

The British army in 1879 was small and professional. Men enlisted for twelve years of service (with the option of re-enlisting for a further nine), and had to be between eighteen and twenty-five years old, fit and unmarried. Their pay compared favourably with labourers' wages. Privates were the lowest and most numerous rank. Above them came the NCOs (non-commissioned officers), rising through corporal, sergeant to colour- or staff-sergeant.

From 1871 officers, who ranked above NCOs, no longer purchased their commissions (signed authorizations by the Queen conferring authority), but were appointed and promoted through examinations, long service and merit. Service extended for thirty years. General officers (field-marshals, generals, lieutenant-generals and major-generals) were responsible for all the troops within their command. Their staff assisted them and conveyed orders to the troops. Below them came the field officers (colonels, lieutenant-colonels and majors); then company officers (captains, lieutenants and sub-lieutenants). Officers have been referred to in this book by their brevet (or army) rather than their regimental rank.

In the following description of the British troops involved at Ulundi, two points must be noted:

1. The given strength of a formation is the ideal. In reality, none of the units would have been up to their full strength. Besides losses through illness or combat, numbers would have been detached to guard forts and laagers and to escort convoys of supplies. For the precise numbers engaged in the battle, see the diagram of the British square.

2. No tropical uniforms were issued to British troops in 1879. The only concession to the climate of Africa was the foreign service helmet, which replaced the elaborate and varied head-dresses worn in Europe. It was made of cork, and was covered with white canvas which was often stained dark on campaign. By July 1879 the bright scarlet and blue uniforms issued to the troops would have been very much the worse for wear — faded, tattered and incomplete.

CAVALRY

A cavalry regiment in the field consisted of 8 troops (or 4 squadrons) made up of 31 officers, 622 men, and 615 horses. It was accompanied by 9 wagons for stores and equipment and 1 ammunition-cart. Elements of two cavalry regiments were engaged at Ulundi. The 1st Dragoon Guards wore scarlet tunics with blue facings, and blue breeches. They were armed with a breech-loading Martini-Henry carbine rifle and a sword. The 17th (Duke of Cambridge's Own) Lancers had dark blue uniforms with white trim, and carried a 3 m long bamboo lance with steel head, sword and pistol.

ROYAL ARTILLERY

A battery of field artillery consisted of 7 officers, 167 men, 132 horses, 6 guns and 16 ammunition and supply wagons. Uniforms were dark blue with red facings. The batteries represented at Ulundi were: 10th and 11th Batteries, 7th RA; Battery N, 5th RA; and Battery N, 6th RA. The first three of these were incomplete, as two 7-pounder guns were at Fort Marshall, two more at Fort Evelyn, and two Gatling guns at Fort Newdigate. This left six 9-pounder guns, six 7-pounder guns and two Gatling guns. The maximum range of a 9-pounder was 3 231 m, and of a 7-pounder 2 862 m. While these guns fired explosive shells, the Gatling gun fired bullets at a rate of up to 400 rounds a minute from its ten barrels. It had an effective range of 1 108 m. Rockets with explosive heads were difficult to aim and had an effective range of 2 055 m.

ROYAL ENGINEERS

A company of Engineers attached to a field force consisted of 6 officers and 196 men. Uniform was a scarlet tunic with blue facings and blue trousers. Engineers designed and constructed military works, like forts.

INFANTRY

An infantry regiment consisted normally of either one or two battalions. A battalion was made up of 30 officers and 866 men, or 8 companies with 3 officers and 107 men to a company. It was accompanied by 3 ammunition carts and 11 wagons for stores and equipment. Uniform was a scarlet tunic (the colour of the facings varying with each regiment) and dark blue trousers. Each soldier carried 70 rounds of ammunition for his breech-loading Martini-Henry rifle, which could fire over 20 rounds a minute with an effective range of up to 1 000 m. The rifle could be fitted with a long sword bayonet for hand-to-hand fighting. Those regiments represented at Ulundi were the 1st Battalion, 13th Light Infantry; the 2nd Battalion, 21st Royal Scots Fusiliers; the 58th (Rutlandshire) Regiment; the 80th Regiment (Staffordshire Volunteers); the 90th Light Infantry; and the 94th Regiment.

MOUNTED INFANTRY

Drawn from the infantry battalions, the men wore their regimental tunics with cord breeches and carried their rifles. Numbers depended on local requirements.

MEDICAL SERVICES

Men of the Army Medical Department detached for service with the Second Division wore scarlet tunics and blue trousers; while the uniform of the detachment from the Army Hospital Corps with the Flying Column was blue with scarlet trim.

RECRUITMENT OF COLONIAL TROOPS

Regular British troops were not sufficient for the invasion of Zululand and it was necessary to recruit from the local population.

NATAL NATIVE CONTINGENT

The NNC consisted of Africans from the 'Native' Reserves of Natal, drafted by local white magistrates, and put under white officers. Only about one in ten had a firearm (and that generally of an inferior muzzle-loading variety), while the rest carried the traditional shield and assegai. They had no special uniform, and were distinguished from the Zulu only by a red rag around their heads. Their job was primarily to go on convoy and garrison duty, to scout for the enemy and to do menial tasks about the camp. Their morale was not good, and they were not expected to fight in the front line. The 2nd Battalion was present at Ulundi.

WOOD'S IRREGULARS

Their function was the same as the NNC but, having been recruited in north-western Zululand from men trained in the Zulu military system rather than drafted in Natal, their morale was reasonable.

NATAL NATIVE PIONEERS

Recruited from the Reserves to assist the Royal Engineers, they wore a scarlet tunic and white trousers.

IRREGULAR CAVALRY

Lack of regular British cavalry for patrol work led to the raising of irregular units from among both white and black volunteers in South Africa. None of these units was much larger than a squadron or about 160 men. They were well trained and of good morale, and carried either the Snider or Swinburne-Henry breech-loading carbine. Apart from the Frontier Light Horse and Natal Light Horse, whose officers wore black uniforms and men buff-coloured ones, they tended to wear ordinary riding-clothes and large hats. Shepstone's Native Horse and Bettington's Horse were with Second Division at Ulundi; while the Frontier Light Horse, Natal Light Horse, Raaf's Rangers, Baker's Horse, and Natal Native Horse were with the Flying Column.

The Zulu Army at the Battle of Ulundi

The Zulu army was not a professional one as was the British. Almost all Zulu men served in it, but only for part of their time. The Zulu military system was based on the *ibutho*, or age-grade regiment. Periodically boys between the ages of fourteen and eighteen would gather at the *amakhanda*, or military homesteads, in various parts of the kingdom. They would serve there for two to three years, herding cattle, working in the fields, and learning military skills. Once there were sufficient boys of an age-group at the various *amakhanda* they would be brought before the king, who formed them into an *ibutho* with its own name with orders to build a new *ikhanda*. For seven to eight months after their formation a new *ibutho* would serve the king in one of the *amakhanda* concentrated in the Mahlabathini plain. Thereafter its members would only go there for the national festivals or on mobilization for war. Otherwise, they would split up, and for a few months a year they would serve in the district *amakhanda*, which they shared with local elements of other *amabutho*.

When serving the king at an *ikhanda*, members of an *ibutho* kept it in repair, looked after the royal cattle and cultivated the king's land. Besides making up the army in time of war, the *amabutho* also acted as the king's police force and did him other services like building him a new homestead.

The *ibutho* was made up of a number of sections, or *amaviyo*. Each seems to have consisted of men of the same age-group from a particular locality, formed during their days as cadets at a district *ikhanda*. The strength of an *iviyo* was normally about 50 men, though it could be as much as 200. There was no fixed number of *amaviyo* in an *ibutho*, which might be anything between a few hundred or a few thousand strong. Its size seems to have depended on the degree of favour in which it was held by the king, and the trouble he took to keep it up to strength.

An *induna* commanded each *ibutho*, with a second-in-command and two wing officers. There were at least two junior officers to each *iviyo*.

Very lavish festival dress distinguished the *amabutho* from each other. On active service, however, much of this was laid aside, though some decorative items like feathers might be retained. Each soldier carried a cow-hide shield, two-thirds the height of a man. *Amabutho* which had received the king's permission to marry carried shields which were mainly white, and unmarried *amabutho* had black or reddish ones. A warrior was armed with a stabbing-spear and normally a few throwing-spears and a knobkerrie or war-axe as well. By 1879 many also had firearms, though most of these were muskets and other obsolete forms of muzzle-loaders traded through Natal and Delagoa Bay. At the battle of Ulundi they also had about 800 Martini-Henry rifles captured at Isandlwana.

In time of war, the scattered local elements of an *ibutho* would be mobilized at their district *amakhanda* and would then proceed to the king in the Mahlabathini plain, where they formed up as a unit. Not all elements of an *ibutho* would necessarily be called up or arrive, so some *amabutho* would be in greater strength than others. Before going into battle all the *amabutho* would be ritually cleansed and strengthened. After combat a Zulu *impi* (or army) normally broke up for the men to be ritually cleansed and to resume their place in the economy of the kingdom.

Elements of all the *amabutho* were apparently present at Ulundi, though those there in their fullest strength seem to have been the uDloko, uMxhapho, iNsukamngeni, uDududu, iQwa, uNokhenke, iNdlondlo, uMcijo, iNgobamakhosi, uVe, uThulwana, iNdluyengwe, iSangqu, iMbube and uMbonambi.

Chapter One

WARDING OFF THE BRITISH

As the early morning mist rose from the Mahlabathini plain on 4 July 1879, the Zulu army moved in to attack the British, who were formed up in a hollow square as if to repel cavalry. There, in the very heart of the Zulu kingdom, amidst King Cetshwayo's *amakhanda* (royal military homesteads), the Zulu *amabutho* (age-grade regiments) broke before the concentrated firepower of Lieutentant-General Lord Chelmsford's men. Their flight ended not only the last pitched battle of the campaign, but the tragic war itself, which British imperial interests had forced upon the Zulu people.

The British called the engagement the battle of Ulundi, their form of oNdini, the Zulu name for their king's principal *ikhanda*. By naming the battle after what they considered to be the Zulu 'capital', and thus the strategic objective of their invading armies, they signified that to them it was the climax of the campaign. The Zulu, however, normally referred to it as the battle of kwaNodwengu after the *ikhanda* nearer which it was fought, and also with reference to the old kwaNodwengu nearby, which had been built by King Mpande (King Cetshwayo's father) and where he was buried. Curiously, it was once equally well-known as oCwecweni, the battle of the corrugated-iron sheets. Doubtless, it was the flashing of the bayonets, swords and gun-barrels along the four sides of the compact British formation which gave rise to this impression. The king himself always maintained that the British had fought from behind iron shields, a view genuinely held by many who had taken part in the battle. Indeed, some went so far as to insist that the British had hung their red coats on iron palings in front of them, off which the Zulu bullets had harmlessly bounced.

All such tales were perhaps necessary for the Zulu to explain why they, having caught the British in the open, away from their forts and entrenched laagers, had yet been unable to overcome them.

There is a tendency among historians today to minimize the significance of the battle. The British were determined to wipe out the humiliation of Isandlwana with a crushing victory of their own which would help restore the image of white invincibility among the black people of southern Africa. It is therefore said that Ulundi was elevated by the British for propaganda purposes to the status of a great victory, despite its being a halfhearted encounter in comparison with earlier battles of the war. Moreover, it is contended that the Zulu defeat in the field did not end the war, as has been conventionally accepted. Rather, the rapid winding-down of hostilities in the weeks following the battle was the consequence of the desire on both sides to have a rapid end to the war, and of the lenient British peace terms which made submission acceptable to the Zulu.

Though there is some truth to this argument, it under-estimates the widespread consequences that can result from a military encounter. There is more than enough evidence to show that this final overthrow of his army was fatal for the king's authority, as his men were no longer prepared to fight on in his defence. This is not to say that they had not fought with great courage and determination, dying bravely, in the words of the commemorative plaque in the monument marking the position of the British square, 'in defence of the old Zulu order'. But the battle demonstrated conclusively that military victory against the British was not possible, and that the overthrow of the Zulu state had to be accepted.

It was for this objective, of course, that the British had gone to war with the Zulu kingdom, militarily the most powerful black state in southern Africa. In the 1870s British policy in the region was aimed at the creation of a confederation of white states. Yet Zululand seemed to pose a threat to this scheme. British officials saw it as the moving spirit of a black conspiracy forming to throw off white rule in the sub-continent, besides posing a standing threat to the neighbouring colonies of Natal and the Transvaal. It seemed that the only way to eliminate the Zulu 'menace' was to dismantle the so-called Zulu 'military system', through which the king directed the productive and military potential of his subjects. The *amabutho* performed many services for the king. They served at the *amakhanda*, keeping them in repair, attending the royal cattle and cultivating the land. In times of peace they acted as the king's police, and at times of war they formed the army.

As it was most unlikely that the king would consent without a fight to the elimination of the basis of his power and authority, or his subjects to the destruction of the very structure of their society, the British prepared to invade Zululand to enforce their will. After months of mounting tension and unacceptable demands, three British columns marched into Zululand on 11 January 1879. The Centre Column with Lord Chelmsford crossed into Zululand at Rorke's Drift, Colonel Pearson's Right Column advanced up the coast, while the Left Column under Colonel Wood entered Zululand from the Transvaal. The plan was that all three should converge on oNdini.

The British made it clear that they were not prepared to negotiate with the Zulu king until they had achieved their objectives of breaking his army in the field and compelling his unconditional acceptance of their terms. At the same time, the British were aware of existing rivalries and tensions among the rulers of Zululand. They knew that some influential chiefs were opposed to the war and hoped for accommodation with the British. Thus while insisting on the destruction of the king's power, the British tried to detach the chiefs from their loyalty to Cetshwayo by appealing to their personal ambitions or their fears of British reprisals.

The Zulu army in action. (*The Graphic*, 3 May 1879.)

The Zulu victory over the Centre Column at the battle of Isandlwana on 22 January destroyed any possibility of a compromise peace settlement. British plans for a quick and successful campaign might lie in ruins with their forces being thrown on the defensive, but their objectives had now to be achieved at all costs. Only the destruction of the Zulu army and state could satisfy them. There was a lull while the discomfited British regrouped and waited for reinforcements. Then on 2 April Chelmsford's column, marching to relieve Pearson's column blockaded at Eshowe, defeated the Zulu at Gingindlovu; while on 29 March Colonel Wood in north-western Zululand routed the veterans of Isandlwana, whom the king had sent against Wood's camp at Khambula, after a bitter and hard-fought battle. The Zulu armies dispersed to their homes to be ritually cleansed, to recuperate, and to restore their badly shaken morale.

With the initiative firmly in the hands of the British, the war now entered a new phase. There was another pause while the invaders gathered their strength for the second invasion. The Second Division of 5 000 men, accompanied by Lord Chelmsford, was to join up with Wood's Flying Column of 3 200 men and to advance on oNdini from the north-west; while at the same time General Crealock's First Division of 7 500 men moved up the coast to the same objective. By the third week of June the Second Division and the Flying Column were in distant view of oNdini from the region of Babanango, though the First Division, bedevilled with supply and transport problems, was no further than the Mlalazi plain. Except for a few light skirmishes, there was little Zulu opposition. For as the war turned decisively against the Zulu king, loyalty to him began to waver, and the British made every effort to encourage the chiefs to accept their terms. By June all the major coastal chiefs were negotiating with Crealock, and many were to submit even before the battle of Ulundi was fought.

Against this background of accelerating desertion, especially in the coastal plain, King Cetshwayo made desperate efforts to ward off the enemy converging upon him. A member of the iNgobamakhosi *ibutho*, whom a patrol from the Flying Column captured on 15 June, told the British that the king had informed his warriors that he was in communication with the British columns regarding terms of peace, but that as they continued to advance on him, and as he was uncertain if the negotiations would come to anything, that he had decided to attack them if they came on as far as the thornveld between the Mthonjaneni heights and oNdini. Despite intelligence gathered by the First Division, which indicated that the king intended to 'eat up' that column before turning his attention to Chelmsford's force, subsequent comment by Cetshwayo himself showed the Flying Column's prisoner to have been correct. After the war, the king told his captors in Cape Town that when Chelmsford's column arrived on the hills south of oNdini, he saw it was impossible for Crealock's column to come up in time. He therefore decided to concentrate on

Chelmsford, and contented himself as regards Crealock with driving as much cattle as possible out of the reach of his patrols.

It is not certain, however, when the king started summoning his *amabutho* for this final stand. Mobilization would take some time, for it was necessary to send the orders by runner or signal to the far corners of the kingdom; and after the defeats of March and April there was a natural reluctance to face the British again, though there were men still prepared to fight if the invaders could be brought out of their entrenched laagers into the open. For the one thing they had learned from their recent failures at Khambula and Gingindlovu was that it was hopeless to attack the British when in prepared positions, be they forts or wagon-laagers.

In early May there were widespread but unfounded rumours reaching the Natal border that the Zulu army was assembling to invade the colony, though it did seem that the king was summoning his chiefs for consultation. By the end of May the Zulu army had not yet reassembled, though there were indications that it was about to do so. Apparently the king had tried to call out his fighting men, but they had insisted that they must remain at home until they had reaped their crops. He had consented, but had ordered that they muster during June. From the coast it was clear to Crealock's patrols that by the end of May the Zulu fighting-men from that part of the country were making for oNdini, despite the fact that many of their chiefs were beginning to negotiate with the British. By early June there was positive intelligence that the king had called up the coastal elements of the *amabutho*, as well as those living along the Natal border and in the upper districts of Zululand, to confront Chelmsford's force. Yet what must have been disturbing for him was the fact that repeated orders had been necessary before his warriors would gather at oNdini again, and there were many reports of their continuing reluctance. Nevertheless, what is significant is that the great majority were still prepared to fight on for their king, despite their lowered morale.

During mid-June, the white trader Cornelius Vijn, who was being taken to the king from northern Zululand where he had been held since the war overtook him, saw nothing but 'troops of Zulus going up continually to the King'. Information from negotiating chiefs and from prisoners confirmed for the British that by the third week of June the Zulu army was assembled at oNdini and the neighbouring *amakhanda* awaiting the king's instructions. From Vijn it would seem that the king was himself at oNdini by about 24 June, and that he was determined to fight the British if necessary in the Mahlabathini plain.

For despite the gathering presence of his army and the deliberate advance of the British, Cetshwayo still entertained some hope of a negotiated end to the war, and redoubled his diplomatic efforts. They were to prove useless, however, for the reality was that the British terms were essentially not negotiable, and the king still wished for a settlement acceptable to him and his councillors. On 5

June Chelmsford told the king's messengers that he would continue his advance on oNdini unless Cetshwayo, to show that he genuinely wanted to negotiate, sent him the oxen of the royal homestead, the two 7-pounder guns the Zulu had captured at Isandlwana, and promised that all the other firearms in Zululand would be collected and given up. In addition, an *ibutho* to be named by Chelmsford must come into the British lines and lay down its arms. Only then was Chelmsford prepared to talk further. The demands were in fact impossible, and demonstrated that Chelmsford was determined to have a battle to avenge Isandlwana. Yet at the same time as he was making it more than difficult for Cetshwayo to negotiate, Chelmsford made it known that chiefs wishing to submit had only to give up their arms and the royal cattle in their keeping, and that their own local positions of power would not be affected. They were to be wooed and the king destroyed.

Officers of the Flying Column. Left to right, sitting: Lt. Henry Lysons, Brig.-Gen. Evelyn Wood, Lt.-Col. Redvers Buller. Standing, from second from left: Capt. Lord William Beresford, Maj. C.F. Clery, Capt. Edward Woodgate.

During its advance Chelmsford's force had met with little resistance. Only the patrols, while engaged in burning every homestead in reach, had the occasional light skirmish. On 26 June, however, as the British approached oNdini along the spine of hills east of Babanango, they came in sight of the *amakhanda* in the Mpembeni valley on the left bank of the White Mfolozi, about 21 km south-west of Cetshwayo's capital. This was a particularly sacred spot for the Zulu as the king's ancestors were buried there. Brigadier-General Wood, with the mounted irregular cavalry of his Flying Column, two squadrons of the 17th Lancers, two 9-pounder guns and two companies of the 2nd Battalion Natal Native Contingent, moved down into the valley (known also as emaKhosini, the burial place of the kings) with the intention of setting fire to the *amakhanda* there, and of outflanking the warriors they saw moving about in them. The guns upset his plan, however, for when they opened fire on the *amakhanda* from long range, the Zulu force of between five and seven hundred men of the uNokhenke and uMxhapho *amabutho* hastily retired. Before they retreated they succeeded themselves in setting three of the *amakhanda* on fire. The British, when they finally came up, burned six more, and noted with satisfaction that they destroyed the 'immense quantities of mielies' stored in them. The burnt *amakhanda*, whose sites are known today, were esiKlebheni, kwaDukuza, kwaKhangela, ezinGwegweni, kwaNobamba and emaKheni. The whereabouts of the remaining three — oDlambedlwini, oQeketheni and ekuDabukeni — have still to be established.

Unbeknown to the British, they had also committed a terrible act of the greatest symbolic importance to the Zulu. At esiKlebheni, where the uNokhenke and uMxhapho were stationed, was kept the *inkatha yezwe yakwaZulu*. The *inkatha* was a circular coil of grass about a metre in diameter, wrapped in python skin and bound with grass rope. It contained the *insila* (or body-dirt) of the king and his predecessors, as well as other ingredients as might be prescribed by the *izinyanga* (medicine-men). Handed down from King Shaka himself, it was the symbol of Zulu unity and very nationhood. It perished in the flames of esiKlebheni, a forewarning of the imminent fall of the Zulu kingdom.

On 27 June the British reached the heights of Mthonjaneni, where the women of King Dingane's *isigodlo* (household) had once drawn clear spring water for him to drink at his emGungundlovu *ikhanda*. The flashing light of the British heliograph alerted the Zulu in the plain below to their arrival, and on that day preparations began to be made for the king to retire to the north. His *isigodlo* girls collected all his personal belongings and stored them in a deep cave in Hlophekhulu mountain, 5 km to the south-east of oNdini. (After Cetshwayo's capture, the men who had helped hide them took possession of them themselves.)

Return of the ambassadors from King Cetshwayo to Lord Chelmsford on 27 June 1879. Note the staffs they are carrying. (*Illustrated London News*, 23 August 1879.)

Meanwhile, a patrol under Lieutenant-Colonel Buller, reconnoitring between Mthonjaneni and the White Mfolozi, encountered the king's messengers Mgcwelo, Mtshibela and Mphokuthwayo bearing two great tusks of ivory, and driving a herd of 150 cattle captured from the British at Isandlwana. Brought before Chelmsford, they made it clear that Cetshwayo could not meet the general's demands of 5 June. Chelmsford declared in that case he would continue his advance, and would not accept the tusks, which symbolized peace. Nevertheless, in order to give King Cetshwayo a last chance to comply with his terms for opening negotiations, he undertook not to cross the Mfolozi immediately, and condescended to keep the cattle as a sign that peace was still a possibility. With that the messengers had to be content. They left the British camp the next day, telling the British interpreter as they went that the Zulu 'would have to fight now' as it was impossible for Cetshwayo to meet Chelmsford's terms, despite his genuine desire to ward off the blow that was descending on him like a falling tree.

Indeed, the final blow could not long be delayed. Lord Chelmsford was by now painfully aware that he had been superseded in his command by Sir Garnet Wolseley, sent out by the British government to end the war with speed and honour. Wolseley was most anxious to be in at the finish, and if Chelmsford wished to win the victory that would wipe out the shame of Isandlwana it would have to be before Wolseley arrived — and he was at the moment hastening from Natal to the front. Moreover, knowing that in the type of colonial warfare he was engaged in that it was imperative to keep the initiative, and to unnerve the enemy by the spectacle of an organized body of troops sweeping inexorably forward, Chelmsford pushed ahead with his preparations for the final confrontation.

Before he could march down into the valley, though, it was first necessary to prepare a strong base at Mthonjaneni, for on 28 June the British had seen a large *impi* (force of armed men) moving below them. Though the British felt this was only a demonstration, they nevertheless could not rule out the possibility that the Zulu intended to attack their base. A cavalry patrol in the direction of the White Mfolozi reported the next day that the *impi* had returned to the king, but later intelligence revealed that three large bodies of Zulu had crossed the river. As a consequence the defences on Mthonjaneni were hurried on. Three extensive wagon-laagers were formed of about 500 wagons and placed in echelon. All the tents, stores and so on were placed inside them, including some 8 000 draught-oxen, and a breastwork was thrown up around the position. The garrison for the post was made up of two companies of the 1/24th Regiment, and 1 NCO and 2 privates drawn from each company in the army. They were to be commiserated with, for the honour of defeating the Zulu would fall to those beginning the long descent from Mthonjaneni.

Chapter Two
AT THE WHITE MFOLOZI

At 8.45 am on the morning of Monday, 30 June 1879, Lord Chelmsford led some 5 500 men out of their camp on the Mthonjaneni heights. The men of Wood's more experienced Flying Column were in advance of the greener troops of Major-General Newdigate's Second Division. The troops were lightly equipped, marching without kits or tents, and with rations for only ten days. Supplies were carried in 200 ox-wagons, and there were mule-carts for the regimental reserve ammunition. As they proceeded some troops engaged in felling trees in the thick thornveld to establish tracks for the advance with wagons four abreast. The *amakhanda* of the Mahlabathini plain came fully into the British view, and cavalry reconnoitring to their front soon spotted three *izimpi*, each about 5 000 strong, on the move towards the river. Their purpose was clearly to guard the drifts should the British attempt to cross. But the invaders did not proceed beyond the base of Mthonjaneni. After a difficult, downhill march of only 8 km they halted at about 3.30 pm by a small stream on the sandy, bush-covered flats, and there formed their encampment.

At midday, while the British were still laboriously on the move down Mthonjaneni, two further messengers from the king, Mfunzi and Nkisimane, encountered Lord Chelmsford. In earnest of the seriousness of their mission they presented the sword taken from the body of the unfortunate Prince Imperial of France, whom the Zulu had killed in a skirmish in June. The emissaries promised moreover the speedy arrival of the two captured 7-pounders and additional cattle. Chelmsford responded by modifying his earlier terms of 27 June somewhat. He now declared himself prepared to accept a thousand rifles captured at Isandlwana instead of the surrender of an *ibutho*. Furthermore, he announced that King Cetshwayo had until noon on 3 July to comply with his conditions. Until that moment, he undertook to keep his troops on his side of the White Mfolozi, provided the Zulu did not fire upon them.

Yet in making these concessions Chelmsford was hardly being generous. His terms still remained outside Cetshwayo's ability to fulfil and appear in any case never to have been considered by the king; while the general's declaration of a truce was to his own advantage. The long grass, boulders, aloes and thorns

The British advance on the White Mfolozi. Note the wagon laager and the bluff just beyond commanding the drift. The fort was built on the hill in the centre foreground. The Mahlabathini plain is in the distance. (*Illustrated London News*, 30 August 1879.)

at the base of Mthonjaneni made it almost impossible for his cavalry to operate, and he was most concerned that the Zulu might attack his force while strung out on the line of march. Diplomacy, it was intended, would bring the British through the danger, and give them time to complete their preparations in peace. Yet this duplicity was not necessary. Contrary to British expectations, the Zulu were reluctant to attack the advancing column in the thornveld because they anticipated that this would cause the British to form a defensive laager of their wagons, and they hoped to be able to attack them when they were outside such defences. Moreover, they were unwilling to launch an offensive until they were sure of the British position and intentions, for the presence of mounted patrols deterred the Zulu scouts and kept their commanders in the dark.

The British resumed their advance at 7.30 am on the morning of Tuesday, 1 July. The Flying Column again took the lead, preceded by Buller's mounted men. The way was once more through difficult country covered in long grass, euphorbias, thorn-trees and mimosa bush. Considerable labour was required by the troops to clear a track and level the drifts for the wagons to cross. Buller and his men reached the drift across the White Mfolozi at about 10.40 am after a ride of some 14 km. From the vantage-point of a small koppie they were able to watch the Zulu army manoeuvering in the plain beyond. These experienced

KEY

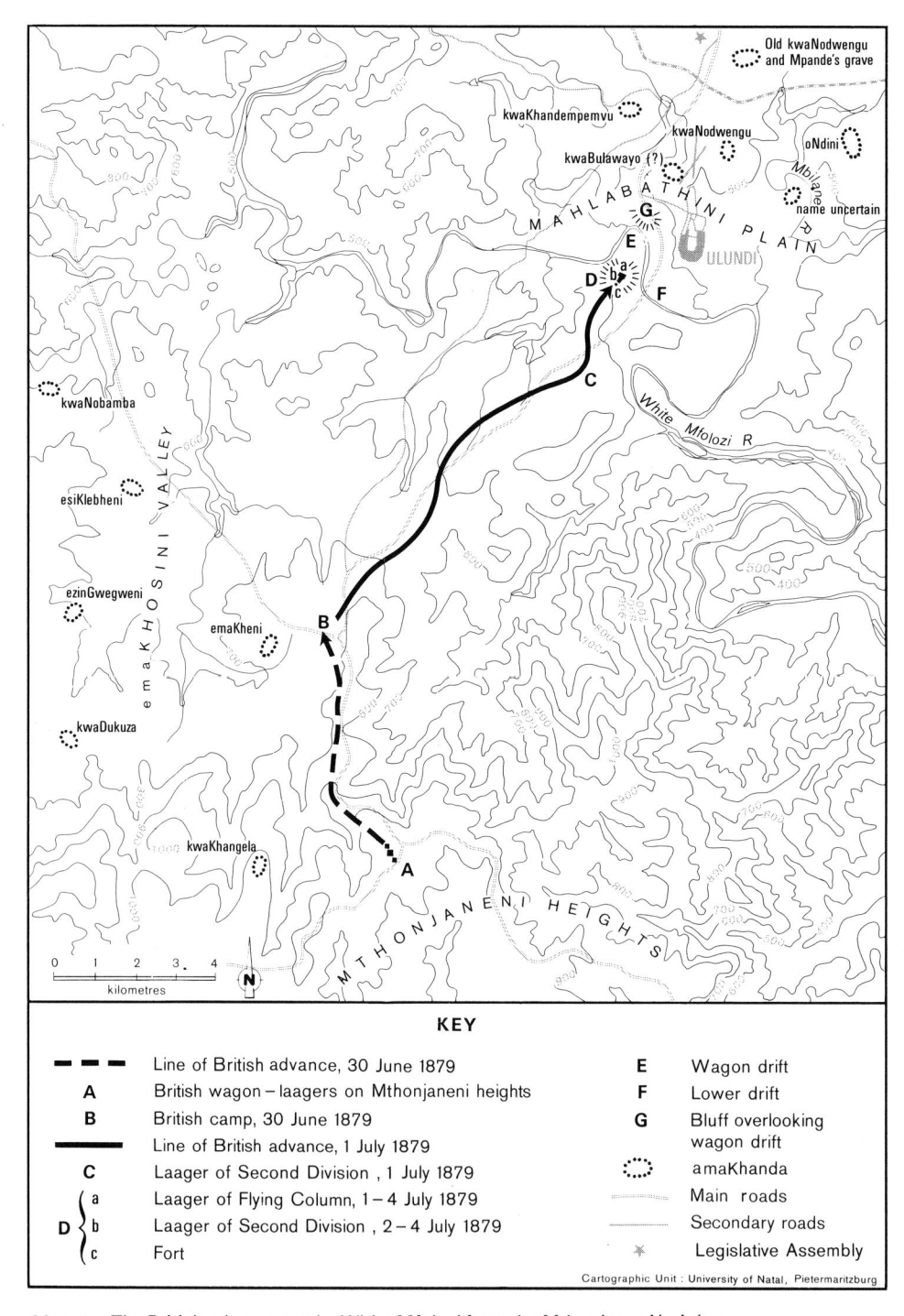

– – –	Line of British advance, 30 June 1879	**E**	Wagon drift
A	British wagon–laagers on Mthonjaneni heights	**F**	Lower drift
B	British camp, 30 June 1879	**G**	Bluff overlooking wagon drift
——	Line of British advance, 1 July 1879		
C	Laager of Second Division, 1 July 1879	⋯	amaKhanda
D { a	Laager of Flying Column, 1–4 July 1879		Main roads
b	Laager of Second Division, 2–4 July 1879		Secondary roads
c	Fort	✳	Legislative Assembly

Cartographic Unit: University of Natal, Pietermaritzburg

Map 1 — The British advance on the White Mfolozi from the Mthonjaneni heights.

men of the Flying Column realized that the Zulu were not forming up for an immediate attack, but were being drilled and doctored (ritually purified and strengthened) in preparation for the fighting to come. Some *amabutho*, about 8 000 strong, came chanting and marching in companies from an *ikhanda* in the extreme north-west of the plain (almost certainly kwaKhandempemvu) and filed into the kwaNodwengu *ikhanda* in splendid order. Soon, the rituals having been completed, they left kwaNodwengu and marched to the *ikhanda* north of it, apparently the old kwaNodwengu. Within half-an-hour four more *amabutho* were seen on the march from various points to the *ikhanda* above oNdini. This was the emLambongwenya *ikhanda*, where the king had gone that morning to address his *amabutho*. There they formed up, filling the space in a huge circle. At about 11.40 am the fighting-men, duly doctored, poured out in three long, broad columns, causing even Buller's veterans to fear for a moment that they did indeed intend to attack. In fact, they need not have been alarmed, for Cetshwayo had instructed his *amabutho* to bar any British attempt to cross the river, but not to fire first upon them. The inexperienced Second Division, however, moving up at the rear of the column, were so alarmed at the 'sounds' emanating from the *amabutho* that they fired blindly on the indignant Flying Column marching in front of them.

Soon after that the Second Division panicked again, in an incident which, like the earlier one, was brushed over in official British accounts. Assistant Quartermaster-General R. Harrison, convinced that the Zulu were not planning an offensive that day, proceeded calmly to choose a camping-ground for the British force in the loop of the river about 1 km from the drift. But before the Flying Column had completed its laager, and while the wagons of the Second Division were still in the road, there was a sudden Zulu movement at about 1.30 pm towards the river. Convinced that an attack was imminent, Chelmsford wildly ordered both laagers to be completed within half an hour. As there was hardly time for this (at least three hours was normally required) Harrison ordered the Second Division to park its wagons on a hill nearly 2 km to the rear of the Flying Column, and for the troops to form up around them and to throw up a breastwork. The Flying Column's laager was already defensible, but the Second Division were thrown into 'great confusion' and had 'a horrible scare'. Despite the British lack of preparedness the Zulu did not come on, and by 5 pm the *amabutho* had all retired to their quarters. This allowed the laagers to be completed normally where they stood, for the bush to be cut down and the grass burnt in a radius of 20 m all around, and for the range-markers to be set up.

That night it poured with rain. For the British, who had not the shelter of huts as had the Zulu across the river, sleep was made no easier by a new panic started in the jumpy Second Division's laager. At about midnight a sentry on outpost duty fired at an officer who had not answered his challenge, which started a stampede to the shelter of the laager among the Natal Native

Contingent who were sleeping outside — as was customary — beyond the abattis (defences made of felled trees and bushes). They did not stop until they had got among the cattle in the centre of the laager, in the process trampling over the soldiers who were sleeping outside the surrounding trench, and the headquarters staff who were just inside the line of wagons.

The following morning, Wednesday 2 July, the Second Division moved forward to park its wagons in triangular formation besides the irregular four-sided laager of the Flying Column, so forming a double laager. The whole of the day was spent in making it secure. The wagons were banked up as high as possible with earth, and thorns and sharp sticks were wedged in, points projecting outwards. The bush was cleared for a 100 m around the laager, and a huge abattis of thorn-trees made. A small stone fort was built on the rising ground at the apex of the Second Division's triangular laager in order to command the position. Its walls, which were made of big stones, were 0,9 m thick and 3 m high. The parapet was formed of felled euphorbias piled on each other and packed with earth. Spare ammunition was to be stored in the fort.

Part of the British camp on the south bank of the White Mfolozi the day before the battle.

The whole position was designed so that a small garrison stationed in the fort and in the Flying Column's laager, with the cattle in the laager between them, could effectively defend the post when the the main force advanced across the river. (The fort, known today as Fort Nolela, is accessible to the tourist.)

While this position was being prepared, other details were busy clearing the way down to the drift. Zibhebhu kaMaphitha, the powerful Mandlakazi chief and *induna* of the uDloko *ibutho*, was a military leader of great resource and dash, and on his own initiative and contrary to the king's instructions, posted marksmen in the rocks on a high bluff overlooking the Mfolozi where the land fell steeply away, just below the drift. From there they opened fire on the troops working at the drift. They also shot at the watering and bathing parties, provoking a lively stampede of naked British soldiers to the safety of their side of the river. It was under this galling but inaccurate fire that Lieutenant Lysons took General Wood's personal escort across the river to retrieve some strayed cattle, and returned with them unscathed. British picquets were now hurried up to return the Zulu fire, and soon pinned the Zulu down behind their rocks. A son of Mnyamana, the Buthelezi chief, and the king's principal adviser, who had gone down to the river with other young men of the *amabutho* to collect wood, was wounded by the British fire.

Despite the exchange of fire at the river, the British continued with the routine of the camp. The band played in the afternoon, and the Zulu were intrigued by the distant sight of companies of soldiers leaving the camp at regular intervals, squatting down in a row, and then returning. They thought it must be a war-rite directed by an *inyanga*(medicine-man), and were only enlightened after the war when they had the opportunity to inspect what turned out to be the British latrine trenches. Feeling much more secure as they fortified their position, the British ceased to be disturbed by the movements of large bodies of Zulu across the river. In the morning these would advance on the river, and having made their show of strength, would return at about 9 am to the vicinity of kwaNodwengu where they would cook a meal before marching off in the direction of oNdini.

Later on 2 July King Cetshwayo made his last effort to negotiate peace terms. He ordered a herd of at least a hundred of the royal oxen to be driven towards the British camp as a sign of submission. But the young men of the uMcijo *ibutho* turned them back, declaring that there should be no surrender while there were still fighting-men left to defend their king. The king, however, was not impressed by the uMcijo's action, for it had taken the final decision whether or not to fight out of his hands. In a powerful speech to his *amabutho* gathered at oNdini he made it clear that he considered the uMcijo's gesture foolhardy, for he had become convinced that the British must win, seeing that the Zulu armies had in the past been unable to stop their advance. Moreover, he voiced his very realistic fear that in defeat his army would disperse, leaving him no option but flight and ultimate capture. At this, his army protested and swore that they would defend him to the last. The king knew better, and sternly warned them that if they did insist on fighting it was now against his advice. But seeing that they were determined to do so, he issued his instructions. They were not to attack the British when stationary, for that would suggest they had entrenched, and bitter experience had shown the consequences of an attack against a prepared position. If they did manage to catch them in the open and defeat them, they were not to pursue the British across the river for the fear of the guns in the laager. So the final battle was not to be avoided, and that night the anxious British saw all around them the camp-fires of the Zulu, eager to prove themselves against the invader.

Soon after daybreak on Thursday, 3 July, Zulu sharpshooters on the bluff commanding the drift again began firing away at watering-parties and bathers, and sent some shots into the laager. One of these snipers was later found by the British to have made himself remarkably comfortable, with straw to sit on, a bough bent over his head for shade, his snuff in a crevice before him, and with a convenient rock on which to rest his rifle. Although a company of the 1/24th answered their fire, the Zulu were too well concealed for this to deter their persistent sniping.

Punctually at noon, when the space Chelmsford had allowed for a reply to his conditions of 30 June had expired, the cattle, which the king had sent in on 27 June as proof of his genuine desire to negotiate, were driven symbolically back across the river. Curiously, the king's messengers of 30 June had refused Chelmsford's request to take these cattle with them. The British believed at the time this was because the cattle had been doctored to ensure their defeat, and that the Zulu feared that if they accepted them back that the magic would be turned on them instead. Whether doctored or not, the return of the cattle signalled the British decision to take the offensive.

For now that all pretence at negotiation was at an end, Chelmsford decided to send a mounted reconnaisance force across the river under the command of Colonel Buller. His objectives were to be three-fold. Almost immediately, he was to drive off the snipers who had been troubling the whole army. Secondly, he was to advance as far as possible along the road to oNdini, to observe the ground most carefully, and to decide where the best position would be for the British to make a stand if the Zulu attacked their advancing force. (In fact, Buller, from Mthonjaneni, had already singled out the gently rolling country to the west of oNdini as the ideal spot for cavalry action against the Zulu.) Finally, he was to provoke the Zulu into responding to his sortie, and so into giving away their points of concentration and plan of attack.

Buller and his approximately 500 mounted men of the Flying Column began their reconnaisance in force at about 1 pm. While a few shells from two 9-pounder guns distracted the Zulu concealed on the bluff, about 100 men under Commandant Baker crossed by the wagon drift and made straight for the Zulu position over the pitted and overgrown ground. The larger part of the force,

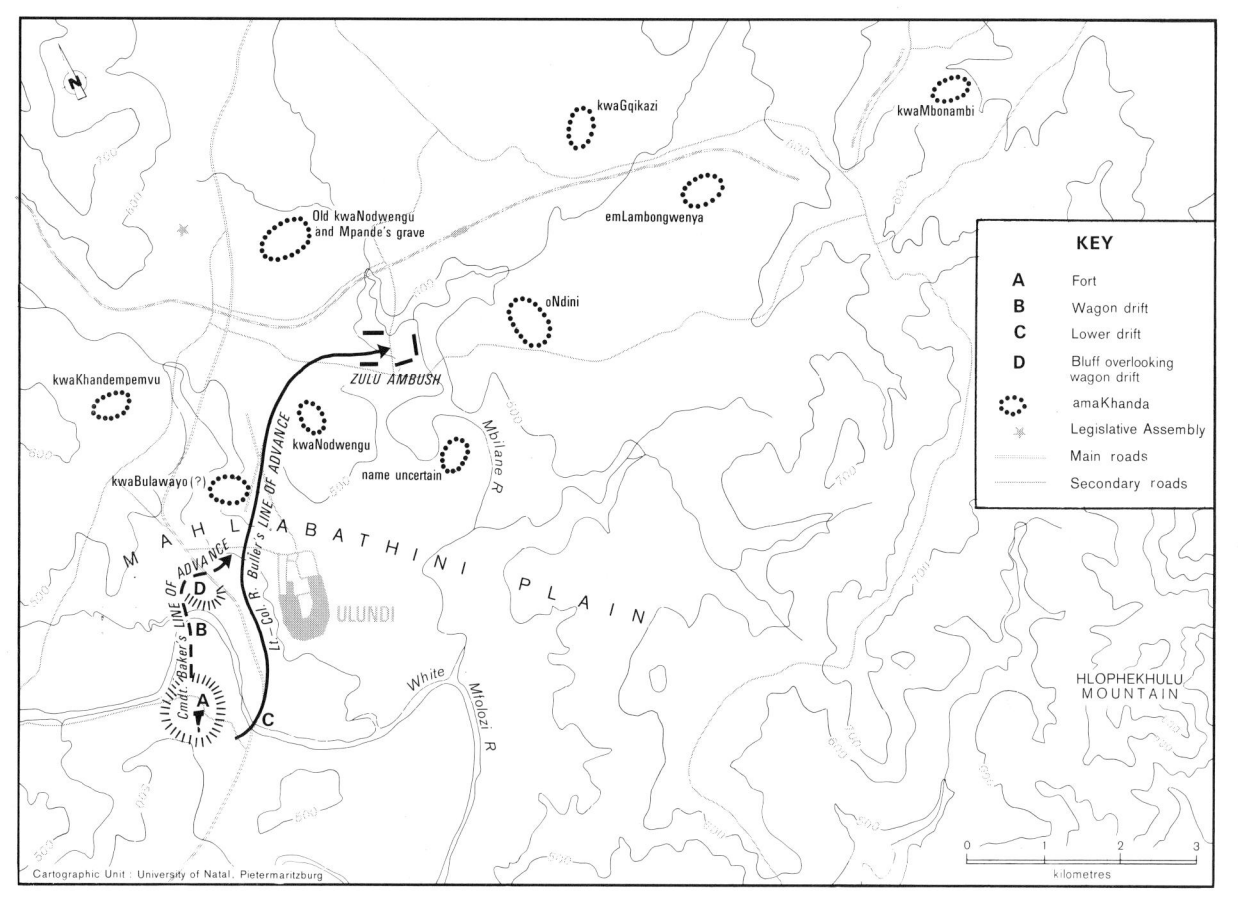

Map 2 — The British reconnaissance of 3 July 1879.

under Buller himself, forded the river at a drift downstream and wheeled to take the position from the south. Buller's men went at a racing pace up the hill, their colonial-bred horses picking their way through the rocky ground with a success the horses of the regular cavalry could never have equalled. Baker's men were the first among the Zulu, who seemed quite taken off their guard, probably having supposed that the two parties had only gone down to the river to water their horses. About 30 Zulu on the crest of the bluff let fly a volley before fleeing, while the rest scattered in all directions from their hiding-places. Baker's men pursued them some way before regrouping. Noting that the Zulu were rapidly concentrating on the surrounding hills, they sent forward a small party to warn Buller, who was in full pursuit across the plain, of the threat to his left rear.

Indeed, Buller was in the process of falling into a most cunningly devised ambush, from which he was most fortunate to extricate his men. When they emerged from the bush near the river onto the open grassy plain, Buller's horsemen encountered some 20 Zulu scouts who had been deliberately placed to lure them on in the direction of kwaNodwengu — exactly where they intended to go anyway. With great skill and courage the Zulu scouts ran before the horsemen, leading them to kwaNodwengu, where other Zulu, driving a large flock of goats, were deployed to draw the British towards oNdini over the ground where the battle was to be fought the next day. Galloping Zulu horsemen, of whom Zibhebhu was one, took up the task and brought Buller's force to the valley of the Mbilane stream, where the ambush was prepared.

About 4 000 Zulu, among whom the uMxhapho were prominent, were concealed in two lines at right-angles to the British right. The long grass near the banks of the stream had been carefully plaited to trip or impede the horse. By this stage, however, the experienced Buller had already begun to sense a trap, and immediately called a halt when his aide-de-camp, Sir T. Hesketh, noticed a Zulu presence in the grass before them. Upon this, the Zulu rose and poured a great volley at the British at about 80 m range. Fortunately for the dismayed horsemen, the Zulu fire was high, and only four saddles were emptied. The British instantly wheeled about, but they were still in grave danger. Two other Zulu forces of between 3 and 4 000 men each had been concealed on both flanks behind the British who had passed unwittingly between them, and now began to close together in an attempt to cut off Buller's escape.

From their fort British lookouts could see what was happening in the plain, and it was causing them the greatest anxiety. Yet Buller was saved by his foresight. He had ordered Commandant Raaf to halt near kwaNodwengu with his horsemen as supports, and they were able to help cover his retreat. Buller's men fell back from the ambush fighting in the Boer fashion. As soon as the front rank became too hotly pressed it cantered to the rear, so that the second rank became the front and repeated the procedure in its turn. Baker's men, who were still near the bluff, supplied cover in their turn, and were supported by fire from the two 9-pounders and from some infantry on the other side of the river. In all, though, Buller was lucky to have reached the drift before the Zulu could cut him off, and only to have lost 3 killed and 4 wounded — though 13 horses were dead or missing.

The experience had been something of a shock to the British. They could not but admit that the Zulu had shown themselves to be excellent strategists, and that they had been extremely well led. In particular they had to admire the professional Zulu skirmishing order as they came down the hill to the ford in pursuit of Buller, and the courageous manner in which, despite the storm of shrapnel and grape-shot from the guns and rifle-fire from the infantry, they had followed the horsemen right down to the river's edge.

For their part, the Zulu were naturally much elated with the near success of their ambush and Buller's hurried flight, and were encouraged to believe that they would have an easy victory should the British venture again into the open. Some Zulu who later came down to the river's edge called out to the British outposts, and with derisive laughs gloated over their victory that day, and promised that none would escape should the British leave the protection of their laager. But as they drank their dram of rum that evening, Buller's men were well content. For one thing, their dangerous sortie had called forth some real acts of gallantry, and had improved the morale of the whole army. Lord William Beresford, Sergeant O'Toole and Commandant Cecil D'Arcy had risked death in turning to rescue troopers who had been unhorsed, and were all subsequently awarded the Victoria Cross. On a more concrete level, the reconnaisance had achieved its principal objectives. Buller had gained an insight into the nature of the country between the Mfolozi and oNdini, and had chosen what seemed the ideal position for the coming battle. (Ironically this spot, just to to the north-east of kwaNodwengu, had also been selected by King Cetshwayo as the place where the British should be brought to battle.) The reconnaisance had had the effect of drawing the Zulu out, and so giving an indication of the strength of the large force concentrated in the plain. But perhaps most important of all, the Zulu had shown what tactics they were likely to adopt when the British advanced across the river again. Their intention would probably be to surround the invaders and cut them off from their base on the opposite bank.

With this detailed intelligence, Chelmsford took the decision to move against the Zulu the following morning. Indeed, if he was to gain the victory he so desired, he had to move at once. That very morning he had received a telegram from Wolseley informing him that his rival and superior was hurrying to the front. So when he issued his orders for the next day, they indicated that he expected his men to finish the work of defeating the Zulu in one day.

For the British, the night before the battle was nerve-racking. It was a bitterly cold night of bright moonlight. Lieutenant Hotham, who had gone to bed at 8 pm, was awakened at about 11 pm by an 'unearthly' sound which seemed at first to be that of distant thunder. It was in fact the noise of the Zulu *amabutho* being doctored for what was to be their last great battle in defence of their kingdom, and soon their dancing and war-songs had the whole British camp awake with the roar of men's voices and the shrill cries of the women. To the startled and apprehensive ears of the British it appeared quite 'fiendish'. It seems some of the singing came from a large contingent who had arrived that very night from the coast and was greeting the king. Blacks with the British force made out some of the words of the songs, the refrains of which consisted of defiance to the British and laments over the men who had fallen that day. It was all enough to make many a British soldier's hair stand on end, feeling as exposed as they did, sleeping in two ranks in a belt around the laagers. There was in addition much movement across the river as the Zulu marched from *ikhanda* to *ikhanda*, and at one point they approached the river, firing off occasional shots. They came so close that individual voices could be picked up. At that point the British thought they were about to be attacked and went on the alert. But the Zulu did not normally fight at night and, still singing, marched away at about midnight, apparently to take up their positions for the

British headquarters, 10 km from oNdini, 3 July 1879: 'Shall we have a fight tomorrow?' (*Illustrated London News*, 6 September 1879.)

next day. Nevertheless, the British cavalry were ordered to saddle up, and by about 2 am were crammed with the oxen in the laager where they spend the rest of the night. Not that the infantry got any more sleep than they, for all expected an attack at daybreak at the latest. British nerves were not calmed at the sight of Zulu campfires and signal lights, not only across the river, but behind them as well. Both sides, the Zulu and the British, could have no doubt that once the sun rose the decisive battle of the war must be fought.

Chapter Three

FORMING UP IN THE PLAIN

The British troops were silently roused from their uneasy dozing at 3.45 am on that fateful Friday, 4 July 1879. They breakfasted on hot coffee and biscuits in the bright moonlight, and then formed up into columns at about 5 am preparatory to crossing the river, over which a slight mist still hung. The total strength of their force was 4 166 white and 958 black soldiers, 12 pieces of artillery and 2 Gatling guns. All the men were provided with two days' cooked rations and carried great-coats in case they had to sleep out. No wagons except those carrying ammunition and entrenching-tools accompanied them. At 5.15 am the bugles sounded a bogus reveille at the normal hour in an attempt to deceive the Zulu into thinking that nothing untoward was in progress.

As day broke the British began their crossing of the river. They left behind them 5 companies of the 1/24th in the laager and 1 company of Royal Engineers in the fort, as well as other small detachments. Colonel W. Bellairs was in command of these 529 white and 93 black troops whose job it was to hold the entrenched camp should the Zulu attempt to take the British base once the main force was committed in the plain.

Buller's mounted irregulars were the first to splash through the river at about 6 am. They crossed by the lower drift and took up position on the bluff overlooking the upper wagon drift by which the rest of the force was to advance. The Flying Column began to cross at 6.20 am and were over by 6.45 am. In their rear the Second Division were across some time after 7 am, moving in parallel column. The regular cavalry brought up the rear. As the troops waded up to their knees across the White Mfolozi they eyed the thickly bushed opposite bank with some apprehension. For although Buller commanded the bluff they still expected the Zulu to oppose them. They need not have been concerned, however. The Zulu plan was to allow the British into the plain and to force them to fight at last in the open, so that they could be destroyed as at Isandlwana. They feared that if they attacked them at the drift before they were committed, that the British would fall back on their impregnable laager.

So the British moved onto the opposite bank without a shot having been fired. About 2,5 km from the drift, when at 7.30 am they had struggled through

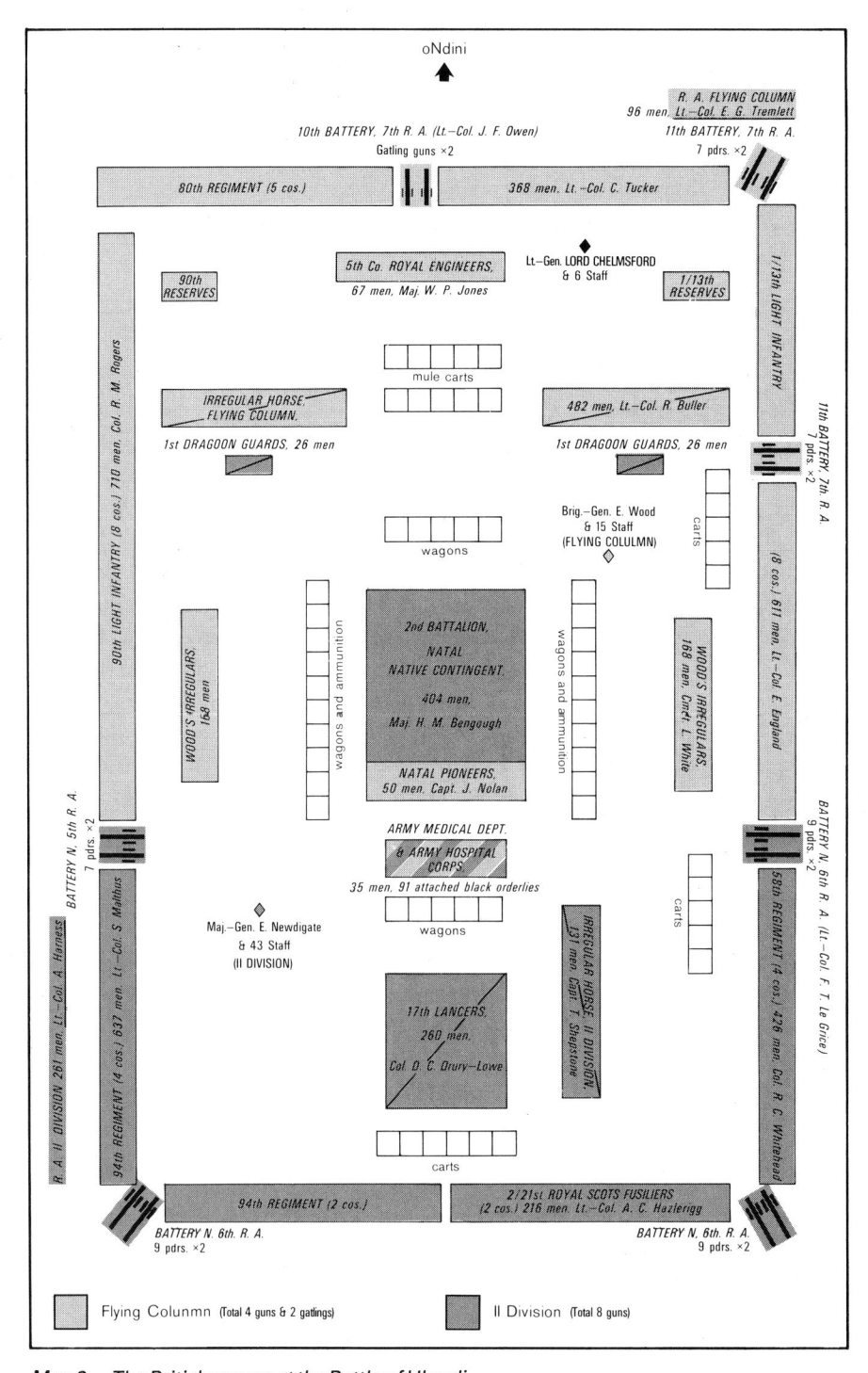

Map 3 — The British square at the Battle of Ulundi.

the rough and bushy ground into the open country, the Flying Column halted with the great circle of huts of what was probably the kwaBulawayo *ikhanda* to their left. While Buller's men continued to reconnoitre in the direction of kwaNodwengu, the Flying Column formed the front half of a hollow square, which was completed by the Second Division marching up behind them. The regular British infantry were ranged four deep, with the guns distributed at the faces and at the angles where the formation was its most vulnerable. At this stage all the mounted men continued outside the square, but reserve companies (who might be required to plug a gap), the Royal Engineers, attached Native Pioneers, the Natal Native Contingent, ammunition-wagons, water-carts, stretchers and medical personnel all took up position inside. After arranging the square, Chelmsford drilled the troops for a while in their formation. Shortly before 8 am the square set off towards the north-east with the Flying Column in the post of honour in the van, following a route between the supposed kwaBulawayo and kwaNodwenga *amakhanda*. Lord Chelmsford rode with his Staff in the rear of the front face of the square, his clear, sharp voice ringing out orders.

Chelmsford's square was already an obsolete military formation, originally devised as an infantry tactic for repelling cavalry. Yet such a shoulder-to-shoulder formation was particularly effective in all-round defence against the likes of the Zulu, who tried to envelope their foes with great rapidity and then to overwhelm them with shock tactics and superior numbers. Isandlwana had demonstrated that a scattered firing-line, even of the most sophisticated weapons, was ineffective against such an attack. On the other hand, the Zulu had little chance against disciplined, concentrated fire by well-drilled troops whose confidence was improved by their tight formation. And once their attack had been broken before the square, they would be vulnerable to a devastating counter-attack by the cavalry. The great draw-back of the square formation—that it presented an easy target for enemy fire—did not apply in Zululand. Zulu marksmanship at Khambula and elsewhere had proved to be poor, and was thus felt to pose no real threat. In the circumstances, there was another advantage, besides the military one, to be gained by adopting the square. On the night before the battle, Wood had called together the men of the Flying Column to tell them that they were going to form a square to demonstrate definitively to the Zulu that they could beat them in the open plain, away from their fortified laager, and that further resistance would be stupid. A British victory would thus ensure the end of the war.

A problem that could not be avoided was that a square was a clumsy formation to manoeuvre intact over any terrain more broken than a parade-ground. Frequent halts were necessary to re-form, and to allow the carts and wagons—which often lagged behind because of the exhaustion of the draft animals—to resume their place in the formation. Moreover, before combat it had to stop to allow the troops to dress ranks and face out. Thus in unavoidably jerky fashion the square proceeded in rather loose formation across the plain where the grass stood 0,6 m high, the Colours of the various regiments flying, and the band of the 1/13th playing stirring music. They were unharrassed by the Zulu. Buller's men were fanned out in advance and about 0,8 km away on the flanks to 'touch' the enemy, while the irregular horse of the Second Division, who made up part of the rear-guard, set light to the kwaBulawayo *ikhanda* as they passed it.

On approaching kwaNodwengu Lord Chelmsford ordered the square to 'half-right turn', so that the *ikhanda* remained on his right flank. To the astonishment of those familiar with the problems of manoeuvering a square, the movement was very credibly performed. The front of the square was now facing oNdini. The British continued to advance for another ten minutes until, at about 8.30 am, the spot Buller had selected on his reconnaissance of the previous day was reached. As the Zulu were now approaching in battle order, the square halted to receive them, manoeuvering slightly to occupy the most favourable part of the ground. The guns were got into position and the ammunition boxes opened. While the men standing in the rear of the four ranks filled the gaps between the men standing in the third rank, the front two ranks kneeled. All fixed their bayonets. Wood's men began to throw up a slight shelter trench outside their part of the battle formation.

The position was ideal for the battle the British hoped to fight. The ground sloped gently down for several hundred metres on every side from the level top of the slight hill giving a perfect field of fire and scope for cavalry pursuit. It was uncommanded from any point, and there was little bush for cover, only the long grass. In that grass Buller's men found the naked corpses of their comrades who had died in the reconnaissance the day before, and whom the Zulu had ritually disemboweled, as was their normal practice. The British hastily buried them, their chaplain reading the burial service in the precincts of a ruined Norwegian mission just in front of their position. The mission's remains were then pulled down to open the range.

When at daybreak the Zulu saw the British crossing the White Mfolozi in force without great numbers of wagons with which to form a defensive laager, they thought that the invaders must have taken leave of their senses so to deliver themselves into their hands. The necessarily slow and deliberate advance of the British square gave the Zulu time, moreover, to develop their strategy. Not a Zulu showed himself to the British until some allowed themselves to be spotted in a donga 0,8 km from the river, after which they drew Buller's men from each donga to the next. For it was the Zulu intention to repeat their ploy of the day before, and to lure the square to the battleground of their choosing between kwaNodwengu and oNdini where they intended to surround and annihilate it. Perhaps the British were right to have believed that the Zulu would have been wiser to have attacked them while they were busy forming their square, or were still in the broken ground unsuitable for cavalry, but that was not the Zulu plan. In fact, it was only at about 8 am, as they were approaching kwaNodwengu, that the British first saw the Zulu gathering in any strength, and began to grasp from their movements that it was the Zulu intention to envelop them, as they had supposed it would be.

To the west an estimated 6 *amaviyo* (companies, of an estimated average strength of 80 men each) were collecting, and 12 *amaviyo* were forming 1 500 m to the north. These bodies continued to swell as they were joined by fighting-men streaming out of the *amakhanda*, so that the British were acutely conscious of the dark clusters of Zulu lining the crests of the hilltops to their left. The Zulu, moving at first in a straggling column parallel to the British square, began to form up in good order for the attack; while to the east, in the stream-beds of the thornveld around oNdini, great masses began to appear through the early morning mists and the smoke from their campfires which had previously obscured them. The Zulu on the hills and in the thornveld to the left, front and right of the British square first joined up to create a great horse-shoe formation, and then at about 8.20 am the concentration in the thornveld extended at the double to pass around kwaNodwengu to the rear of the British square, and so to complete a great circle around it, over 14 km in length.

While the British were advancing towards kwaNodwengu, two Zulu forces, perhaps about 5 000 strong, were moving out of an *ikhanda* near the river to the right of them (whose name it has been impossible to establish) in the direction of the entrenched camp across the Mfolozi. It is conceivable that their intention had been to dispute the British crossing and that they had been caught unawares by their early start, but it is most likely that their purpose was to capture the British base and cut off the square's retreat. At 8.10 am the two *izimpi* came close enough to the drift for the garrison of the post to go on the alert, and some Zulu even crossed the river and came to within 500 m of the laager. However, they never seriously threatened the garrison, and the two *izimpi* soon melted away to join the battle developing in the plain.

There, the British watching the Zulu advance could only wonder at the skill and timing which, considering the difficult terrain and the varying distances they had to cover, allowed the Zulu units to synchronize their envelopment. As the Zulu moved down the slopes towards them, they appeared at first to the apprehensive British to be almost indistinguishable from the aloes that covered the slopes. It was soon apparent, though, that the Zulu were closing in, keeping the most 'splendid order' in loose undulating lines of companies about four deep, with intervals between the *amabutho*, followed by others in file to the rear. They were preceded by irregular waves of skirmishers (just as 'modern tactics' required, the admiring British realized), who opened a desultory fire at a great distance. In all, the Zulu advance was a revelation to the British, who had been led to expect a rush from dense, irregular masses, instead of the 'beautiful', 'splendid manoeuvering' in half-open order they were witnessing.

The size of this Zulu army converging on the British is a matter for some debate. Contemporaries could not agree on a figure. The official British estimation was 20 000. Captain Offy Shepstone considered that there was a total of 25 000 Zulu present, although 8 000, who were older men, never came under fire. On the other hand, the newspaper correspondent, Archibald Forbes, felt that only 10 000 Zulu were engaged. This figure is closer to that of Major Ashe and Captain Wyatt Edgell, who put theirs at 15 000 engaged and 8 000 in reserve, very near that of the other newspaper correspondent, Charles Norris-Newman's minimum of 15 000 engaged and 5 000 reserves. Captain McSwiney, on the other hand, opted for 25 000, though Lieutenant Hotham's 30 000 is an obvious exaggeration. Captain Slade's maximum of 16 000 is nearer again to Forbe's conservative estimation. Frances Colenso concluded very sensibly that as the Zulu army had gathered from over such a large area, and as some *amabutho* had suffered severely in earlier engagements, that it was almost impossible to arrive at any reliable conclusion as to its size. Her reservations seem to be borne out by the intelligence that fewer of the Zulu along the Natal border took part in the call-up before the battle than for Khambula, and that their casualties were also considerably less. King Cetshwayo himself declared that all his *amabutho* were represented at the battle, and that the army was about the same size as that which had fought at Isandlwana, which is estimated at 20 000 strong. Although Chelmsford would have liked to believe reports that it was greater than the army assembled for Khambula, which was probably rather in excess of 20 000 men, the Zulu army on 4 July was probably between 15 000 and 20 000 strong, with over 5 000 in reserve. Greater precision is not possible.

Despite reports to the contrary, the king was not in personal command of his army on the day. Having instructed his generals, he had left oNdini on the evening of 3 July, and travelled with his *isigodlo* to the emLambongwenya *ikhanda* of his father Mpande. The iNdabakawombe *ibutho* acted as escort. Early the next morning messengers arrived with the news that the British were advancing across the river. On learning this, the king moved further away to his kwaMbonambi *ikhanda*, followed later by his *isigodlo*. He was there throughout the battle, and had look-outs posted to give him news of the outcome. Ziwedu kaMpande, his favourite brother, who stood in status among the princes second only to Hamu (who had betrayed the king and gone over to the British), watched the battle from the Mcungi hill in the company of other of the king's brothers and many of the great chiefs. It was Ziwedu's presence which was mistaken for that of the king's in many accounts.

Who were the other commanders present? The British compiled lists of those most likely to have been there, such as Mnyamana, Ntshingwayo, Dabulamanzi and Sihayo. But despite the British concern to establish the presence of Zulu leaders to whom they attached particular notoriety, proof is lacking. Dabulamanzi, for example, was clearly on the coast under the king's surveillance because he was in the process of attempting to submit to Crealock, and was therefore unlikely to have been at the battle; while as for Mnyamana, it is known that he left the king on the morning of 4 July and rejoined him after the battle, so it is possible but unproven that he was with Ziwedu. As with Mnyamana, it is likely that other chiefs such as Ntshingwayo, Sihayo and his son Mehlokazulu, Qethuka kaManqondo, Mtuzwa, brother of Sekethwayo the Mdlalose chief and Mundula, the *induna* of kwaNodwengu — all of whom were reported to have attended a royal council on 2 July — witnessed the battle. None of them, however, came prominently to the fore during its course. Yet there was nothing unusual about this, for it was normal Zulu practice for high-ranking officers to station themselves on a vantage-point some distance from the actual conflict. In the event, therefore, besides Ziwedu, whose presence is established, it is impossible to be sure who the other major Zulu commanders were, let along their subordinates.

There is more certainty over the actual Zulu order of battle, though the problems posed by lack of detailed evidence comparable to that concerning the stationing of the British troops for battle must be remembered. Ulundi presents special difficulties because of the numbers hanging back as uncommitted reserves. It should also be borne in mind that as an attack was pressed home *amabutho* naturally lost formation and became intermingled, making the positive identification of their positions even more uncertain. In the end, the most authoritative analysis that survives is that compiled by Captain Edward Woodgate, Wood's Staff Officer, from his own observation and from information gained from prisoners. The uDloko *ibutho* came straight at the front of the British square. The encircling left horn consisted of the uThulwana, iNdluyengwe, iSangqu and iMbube, and there is positive reference elsewhere to the uMbonambi. The Zulu right horn was made up of the uMxhapho, iNsukamngeni, uDududu, iQwa, uNokhenke and iNdlondlo *amabutho*. The iNgobamakhosi and uVe attacked the right rear of the square, and the uMcijo the left rear. It seems Thonga auxiliaries were also present. These, then, were the units most obviously involved. Elements of the other *amabutho* either went unregarded because they were few in number, or made up the reserves which never properly joined the attack on the square.

Chapter Four
THE BATTLE

The mist was slowly lifting from the hills, but still hung above the river. Between the stationary red square in the middle of the plain and the long lines of advancing Zulu were scattered bodies of horsemen, standing in line. In meeting the imminent attack of the Zulu army, the British intended to resort to what were, in the circumstances, standard tactics.

The square is a defensive formation, dependent on a great rate and concentration of fire which will mow down an enemy charge and bring it to a standstill before getting close enough for hand-to-hand combat. But for fire to be effective, it is necessary to reserve it until the enemy is well into range. And Chelmsford would have known that the loss caused by small-arm fire to relatively undisciplined troops advancing in open order was actually slight, and that it was essential therefore that shooting be accurate and well-disciplined. To open fire too early would be ineffective, and might have the additional disadvantage of scaring off the enemy before the full effect could be felt, and so ruining the chance of a decisive victory. The objective, then, was to tempt the Zulu into effective range. The case of Khambula had already demonstrated how effective irregular cavalry could be as a decoy, especially in provoking unco-ordinated charges that could be dealt with most successfully in turn.

This successful tactic was thus repeated, while the regular cavalry of the Second Division (the 17th Lancers and the small detatchment of Dragoons), who considered the terrain not suitable and the Zulu line too powerful to be charged, entered the rear of the square. Their particular skills would only be of use once the Zulu were in retreat.

Buller's irregular horsemen in front of the square became engaged with the Zulu between 8.35 and 8.45 am. They again followed the Boer mode of combat, fighting in two ranks, retiring alternately. The front rank remained mounted and ready to dash at a weak point in the enemy's line; while the second rank dismounted, using their saddles to rest their rifles.

It was Baker's Horse who first made contact with the Zulu. They advanced towards the left wing of the rapidly closing Zulu formation, which

Drawing on the Zulu attack in the opening stage of the battle of Ulundi. Sketch by Lt. W.F. Fairlie of Shepstone's Horse.

broke up and scattered into skirmishing order when they saw the horsemen coming. Lieutenant Parmenter cantered ahead with about twenty men and poured a volley into the Zulu at about 200 m. Furious at being challenged by so small a body, the Zulu fired at random and rushed forward to try — unsuccessfully — to cut Parmenter off. The admiration of the British, however, was for Captain Cochrane's experienced Natal Native Horse, who were in advance of the right of the square. They fell back slowly and deliberately, pouring volley after volley into the advancing Zulu. They were, in fact, under the impression that they were to remain outside the square, as they had stayed outside Wood's camp at Khambula, skirmishing throughout the battle. Consequently, they only retired reluctantly into the square, where they were bluffly ordered to eat their ration of biscuit and lie down. But their leisurely withdrawal had the effect of hurrying on the Zulu advance. Irritated Zulu called tauntingly after them: 'Gallop on, but we will overtake you. We are going to kill every one of those red men!'

Buller's men were soon heavily engaged on three sides, and the various corps all retired independently towards the square with equal regularity and steadiness, drawing the Zulu on. Captain Shepstone's Horse, who were attached to the Second Division, waited to the left rear of the square for the uMcijo *ibutho* to come on in a great column more than thirty deep, firing wildly, waving their shields and shouting 'uSuthu!' Shepstone's Horse opened fire at a range of 300 m before retiring slowly into the square before the uMcijo. As they fell back the artillery opened fire over their heads. Soon all the horsemen were back in the square, the front and rear faces of which had wheeled outwards to receive them, before closing again to face the Zulu's charge. The battle was about to begin in earnest.

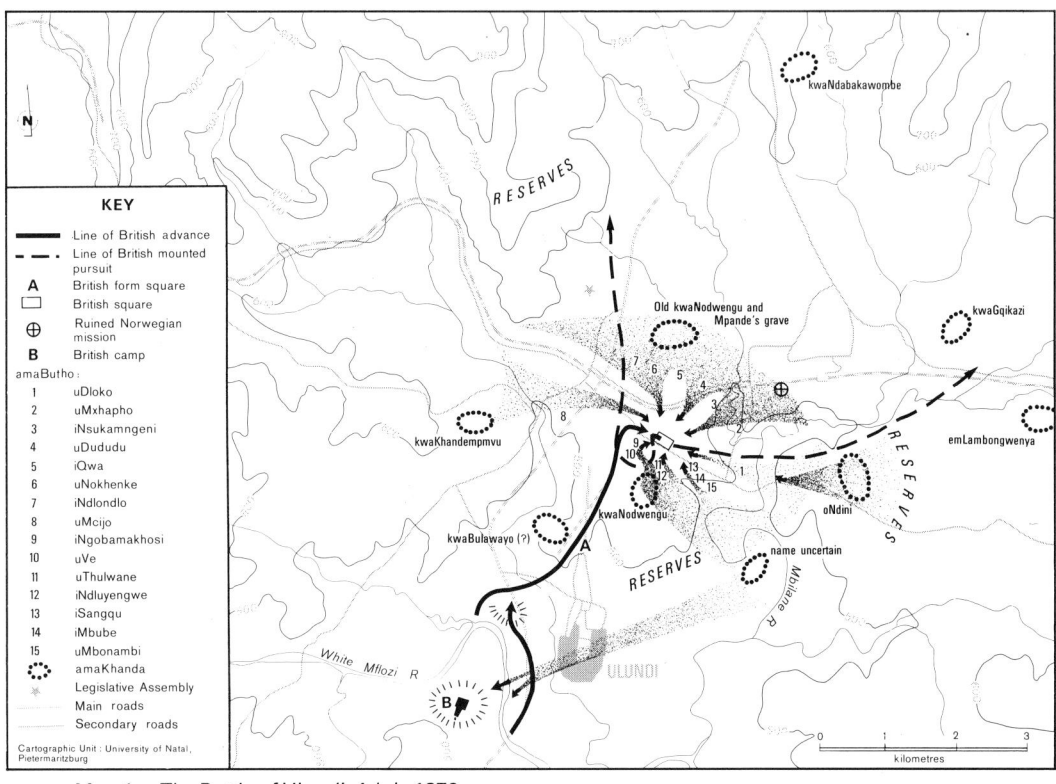

Map 4 — The Battle of Ulundi, 4 July 1879.

The 9-pounder guns fired their first shot at 8.45 am when the Zulu were 1 100 m away. Soon the guns on all four sides, where they were dispersed to meet the Zulu envelopment, were firing away, at this stage from positions just outside the square. The Zulu, because they were mainly in skirmishing order, suffered little damage at first, though some were staggered by the bursting shells, and a few scattered. Perhaps there is some truth in the later comments that the shrapnel 'took the dash' out of the Zulu attack, but this was not immediately apparent. For the Zulu instantly rallied with the intention of rushing in. Their great circle surrounding the square contracted to within the effective range of small-arm fire, so that the guns were joined by the Martini-Henry and Gatling guns. At 8.50 am the fire from the square became general. All sides engaged at a range of about 300 m, though the right face, where the Natal Native Horse had drawn on the Zulu so effectively, came into action a few moments before the others.

The Zulu advanced into this terrible fire still in skirmishing order, but with large masses behind in support. They closed in steadily and in silence, and only uttered their war-cry, '*uSuthu!*' when they were preparing for the final rush. Those who made this desperate charge were stripped for battle of all finery, and were fine, well-made men of the younger *amabutho*. Indeed, the perfect state of their teeth was to be a matter of wonder for the British when they later inspected the dead.

In the main, the Zulu attack brought them no closer than within 70 to 100 m of the British position, though there were individual exceptions, like the young warrior who was shot fruitlessly throwing an assegai at 20 m. But his failure to reach the laager and engage in hand-to-hand combat (as had occurred at Khambula) has encouraged historians like Jeff Guy to assert that the Zulu attack was half-hearted, because the Zulu entertained no hope of success. Certainly, there is some contemporary evidence to support this view. Prisoners were reported to have said that as they were moving to the attack word passed among them: 'What are we marching there for? Only to be killed'. Consequently, many fought without enthusiasm, and others broke away. In this regard the comments of General Wood, the victor of Khambula, have been unduly influential. In his autobiography he unfavourably compared the 'hurried, disorderly manner' in which the *amabutho* came on at Ulundi with their 'methodical, steady order' at Khambula. But Wood was not a disinterested observer, for he was not in command at Ulundi, and clearly wished to minimize Chelmsford's success. It cannot be denied, however, that

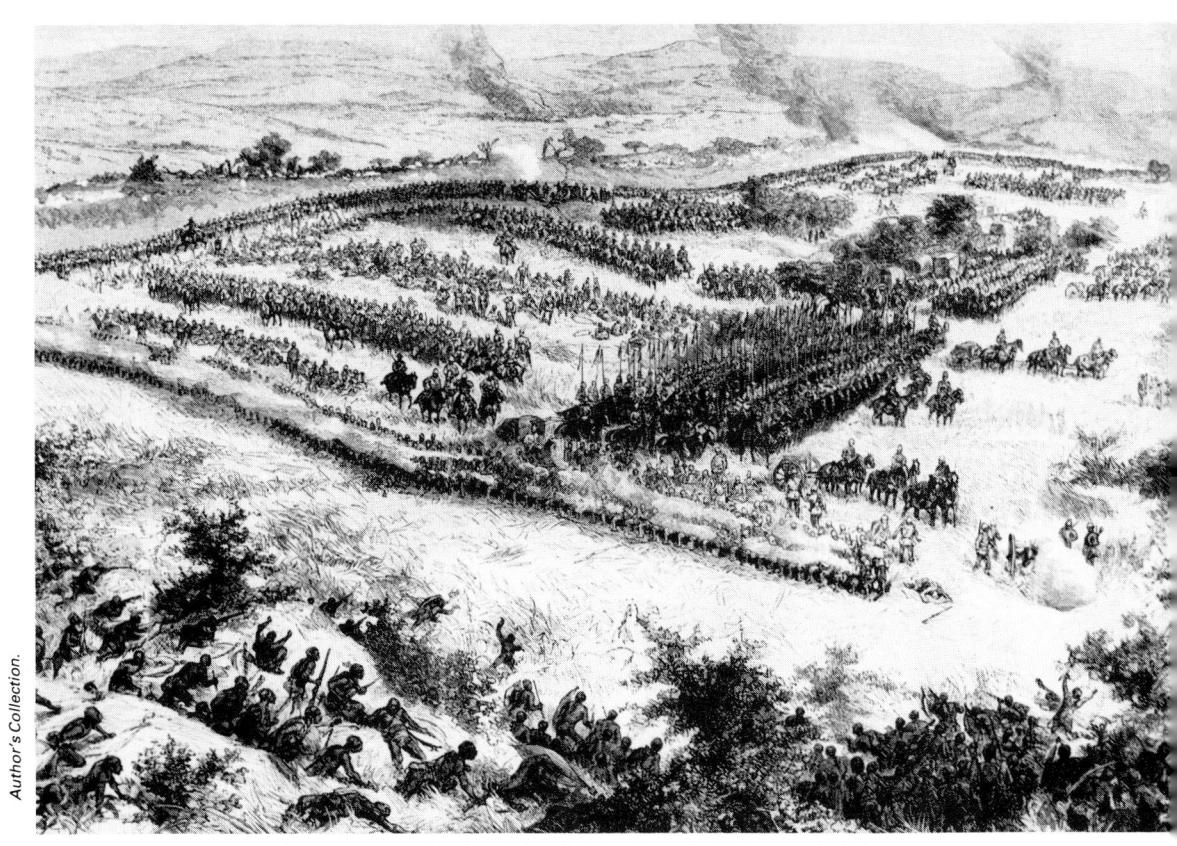

The Zulu engage the British square at the battle of Ulundi. (*The Graphic*, 23 August 1879.)

the Zulu must have learned from their experiences at Khambula in particular, and were thoroughly aware of the effect of British fire at close quarters. Nor is there any doubt that their string of defeats had affected their confidence and shaken their earlier sense of invincibility. Mehlokazulu stated that the Zulu at Ulundi did not fight with 'the same spirit, because we were then frightened'; and further British witnesses commented on their relative lack of determination.

Yet what much of the evidence amounts to is proof that the Zulu had acquired a better appreciation than before of the effectiveness of concentrated fire, and a more realistic sense of when it was pointless to persist in an attack. For there is overwhelming evidence to show that in the initial stages of the battle, before the hopelessness of their task became obvious, that the Zulu came on with 'enormous pluck', advancing with the 'same intrepidity' as at Gingindlovu and Khambula. Indeed, many of the British were simply astonished at the 'amazing courage' of the Zulu, who repeatedly and unflinchingly attempted to charge through the withering fire. Melton Prior of the *Illustrated London News* could only reflect that of all the campaigns in which he had taken part, never before had he come across so courageous a foe, nor one which he had felt more pride in seeing beaten.

The British were confident of their ability to crush the Zulu assault, and the men of the 1/13th were seen beckoning to the Zulu and shouting, 'Come on, you black devils!' Yet how intense or effective was the British fire? The British infantry — and the following figures exclude the colonial mounted units for which there is no tally — fired some 35 000 rounds. This was exclusive of artillery fire, which amounted in its turn to 90 rounds of artillery ammunition and 3 rockets shot at kwaNodwengu. Rounds fired were calculated at between 7 and 6,4 per infantryman. From these statistics Frances Colenso concluded — and she is followed in this by Guy — that there was a low rate of fire, which proves how easily the Zulu were repelled. Colonel C. Callwell, however, pointed out in his official manual on the conduct of 'small wars' that heavy expediture of ammunition was unusual on such campaigns, and that in a typical battle under 10 rounds per man was the norm. Moreover, it should be remembered that it is unrealistic to link ammunition consumption to rate of fire, because none of the men in the square were engaged without pause for the entire battle. Strict fire discipline was practiced, furthermore, and this would have reduced the rate of fire while increasing its accuracy.

If it is accepted, therefore, that the British set up an impenetrable wall of fire in front of whatever section of the square was threatened, it still remains to be questioned how fatal it proved to the Zulu. Despite the steady volley-firing by company, the Zulu were a hard target to hit because of their open order and their wonderful use of what cover was available. Those advancing were seen running in a crouching position behind their shields, while the masses lay in the high grass (the British had only managed to beat down the grass for a few

Lt.-Col. J.F. Owen, R.A. with the Gatling gun he served at the battle of Ulundi.

metres outside their square), and afforded no target to the British except the smoke of their firing. This was most probably the reason for much high volley-firing from the square, which saved the Zulu many casualties. In addition, the volume of smoke aided the Zulu, for the British could not see many metres to their front because of it. What came from the firing of weapons was bad enough, but it was made worse by the billows given off by kwaNodwengu, which the British had set alight as they passed it. So effective was the smoke from the *ikhanda* in screening the Zulu, that Chelmsford had eventually to order the fire there to be extinguished. Every now and again the bugles had to sound the cease-fire to allow the smoke to clear away, and then the Zulu would take advantage of the lull to creep closer and blaze away at the square, from which deliberate and independent firing was allowed between volleys. Nor was the new weapon, the Gatling gun (an early form of machine-gun) as effective as the British might have hoped, though it was recognized that it was capable of causing havoc to the enemy only for so long as it did not jam. During the course of the action the pair in use jammed six times because the bolts slipped out and were difficult to find in the long grass. Their effect was certainly initially demoralizing for the Zulu, who suffered heavy casualties before them (Wood counted 60 dead in the long grass 70 m to their front), though some Zulu got up to within 40 m. In other words, if the Zulu were able to make use of cover to avoid the full effects of the fire at some distance from the square, then they were unable to press with any degree of safety or success into the zone within 100 m of the British firing-line.

It seems extraordinary that in its turn the British square was not more vulnerable to Zulu fire. Most of the Zulu had some form of firearm (in total they probably carried more at Ulundi than the British), even though the majority were inferior muzzle-loaders of some sort. But there were small numbers of modern breech-loaders, including Martini-Henry rifles captured at Isandlwana. And the British square did, after all, present an enormous target. Its interior was crammed with ammunition and water-carts, draft-animals and their drivers, dismounted cavalry and irregular horsemen with their horses, as well as the Natal Native Contingent who, poorly armed, ill-trained and untried in battle, cowered behind the soldiers face downwards with their shields on their backs, crying out in alarm. The Colours of the 1/13th were unfurled, presenting a striking target, while no less vulnerable were the generals and their staffs. Lord Chelmsford refused to dismount, so all remained on horseback throughout the battle. It was a particular wonder that his bravado did not result in more casualties, especially since the Zulu usually fired high. Lord Chelmsford himself directed the musketry fire on a number of occasions, and in all must have toured the square a dozen times during the engagement.

Yet for all that it was an easy target, casualties in the square were very low. The reason, quite simply, must be attributed to poor Zulu marksmanship, though their fire was always most energetic. No sooner had the square taken up

Inside the British square during the battle. (*Illustrated London News*, 23 August 1879.)

its battle position than it had been assailed by a dropping and harmless fire from the distant Zulu, especially those advancing from the direction of oNdini. While they converged on the square in the wake of the irregular cavalry, the Zulu fired and pushed forward alternately in their loose, open order. But that fire was equally ineffective, as was their heavy and continuous firing from their final position around the square, which continued for about half-an-hour. The British were all very conscious of how lucky they were that the Zulu could not shoot more accurately. The fundamental Zulu fault was that they almost all shot too high. The British supposed this high firing to be a consequence of erroneous musketry theory. The Zulu knew that the British raised their rifles sights to fire at long range, and conceivably thought that to do so would increase the velocity of bullets at short range. In all events, what casualties the British suffered were mostly in the rear ranks where the men were wounded in the back as a consequence of Zulu fire coming over the heads of the men on the opposite side of the square. Indeed, there were definite cases of Zulu being hit by fire from their fellows on the far side of the British formation. Some Zulu snipers were more accurate than the mass, though the British were generally able to pick them off, shooting some out of a tree, and silencing a courageous pair who had settled down with a box of Martini-Henry ammunition between them. The British, in other words, were treated to a great deal of smoke and noise from the Zulu guns, and a mainly harmless rain of bullets overhead, each one of which emitted its own distinctive note: the sharp ring of the Martini, the wail of the rough-cast bullets of Enfields and long elephant guns, and the literal howl of the potlegs and wire projectiles.

The Zulu came their nearest to breaking through the ring of British fire and reaching the square at the right rear corner. The angle of a square is its weakest point because it is the most difficult part to cover with effective fire, and because there is more likelihood of confusion in the ranks. The Zulu instinctively grasped this fact. Thus, when the Zulu advancing against the right face of the square from the kwaNodwengu *ikhanda* were checked by British fire at between 400 and 500 m, they changed their tactics and made for the rear right corner. (It should be mentioned that kwaNodwengu served as a rallying-point throughout the battle. As it provided good cover, crowds of Zulu were constantly rushing into it. Some lined the huts and the stockade facing the square and kept up a heavy fire.) The assault from kwaNodwengu, then, veered left up a depression running along the British rear, which gave them complete shelter to within 150 m of the right rear corner. Here they rapidly collected, between about 2 000 and 3 000 strong and 30 ranks deep. Striking their white shields and shouting 'uSuthu!' they charged to within 30 m of the corner, though a few corpses were later found only 9 paces from the British line. So close did they come that Battery N, 6th RA had to fire 7 rounds of case-shot, which is used only at the closest quarters, and several officers drew their swords or revolvers, expecting a hand-to-hand fight. The 5th Company, Royal

Engineers was brought up to reinforce the corner, though this ultimately proved unnecessary. Lord Chelmsford himself was seriously alarmed at the situation, and riding up to the threatened angle called out: 'Men fire faster! Cannot you fire faster?' His request was answered by a storm of fire which checked the Zulu charge, for the British infantry were still managing to remain as cool as if on parade, obeying their officers' orders on sighting and firing in sections. Captain Slade commented that the fire they managed to develop in that crisis was so 'solid and well directed' that no troops in the world could have stood up to it, and marvelled at the way the Zulu nevertheless persisted as long as they did.

The determined and nearly successful assault by what were mainly the iNgobamakhosi and uVe on the right rear corner of the square was not fully matched by that of the uMcijo on the left. Shepstone's Horse had retired before their column of over 30 men deep, which came up in the most determined manner from a hill to the left rear of the British to the cover of a ridge 300 m away. There they were checked by the British fire and deterred from advancing any further in force, though daring individuals came dashing down the slope and, concealed in the grass, crept forward to snipe. Meanwhile, the attack on the British left was pushed forward with such vigour that the infantry were in expectation of hand-to-hand fighting. But there too the Zulu were held. At the front face the Zulu developed their attack where a dip in the ground allowed them to form up in comparative safety. Here too they were checked as they appeared at the crest.

At this stage, with the Zulu assault pinned down at every quarter, the main Zulu reserve, a few thousand strong and apparently made up of members of the older, married *amabutho*, emerged from oNdini. They moved down the slope towards the Mbilane stream in a wide rectangular column 50 deep, beating their shields and shouting their war-cries. Two 9-pounder guns were moved from the left rear to the left front angle (the Gatlings at the front face were jammed), and opened fire at about 2 000 m with shrapnel. The shells burst in front of the Zulu column which opened out into two wings. When a shell fell on each of the wings they hesitated, then closed. Two more shells falling on the reunited column caused it to turn and leave the field. Other reserves, which were posted on the hills to the British left, and between them and the river with the purpose of cutting off the retreat of the square should it break, were consequently not brought up and never came under fire. This immobility may also be partially ascribed to the reserves' heeding of the king's warning not to fight the British if they were stationary, as this was presumed to indicate that they were entrenching their position.

The battle in the plain raged for about half an hour from the time it became general, until at about 9.15 am the Zulu attack began to slacken and then falter. Lieutenant-Colonel Robinson was convinced this was not from any loss of nerve on the Zulu part, but because they were perplexed that they could find no way around or through the British fire. They had doubtless been confident that working around the faces of the square they would eventually have found some opening to exploit (such as the nearly gained right rear corner) through which to overwhelm the British at close quarters.

Yet as success eluded them they began to hesitate; some stopped, while other individuals began to run away. This gradually precipitated a disorderly withdrawal which was underway by 9.20 am, though as yet there was no general rout. For though the Zulu fell back it was not for far, and attempts were made to rally. What must have made their inability to break through the cordon of British fire all the more bitter was their knowledge that they had actually succeeded in their strategy of surrounding the enemy in the open plain.

When the British realized that the Zulu were retiring they ceased fire, and burst into cheers, some men enthusiastically throwing their helmets up into the air. General Wood tried to suppress the hurrahs, for he believed that the Zulu would still try to make a last stand at oNdini. But it was not to be, and the sound of cheering only disheartened the Zulu, convincing some that the battle was indeed lost. Yet for others the British cease-fire was an encouragement. They paused to look back, clearly hoping to see the British formation breaking in pursuit, and so affording them that long-awaited opportunity to close with the invader in hand-to-hand combat. But they were to be disappointed. The left face of the square greeted their momentary halt at 9.25 am with a short burst of firing, and artillery fire broke up every new concentration of Zulu. Demoralization began inevitably to set in and the Zulu retreat gathered momentum. It was now becoming a question of escaping unscathed from the hopeless field, and as they fled the Zulu felt acutely that their 'fighting strength was sinking like the setting sun'.

This was the moment the cavalry had long awaited. Regular troops were unable to deliver an effective counter-attack against an adversary as mobile as the Zulu, but a well timed cavalry charge over the open plain was enough to throw the disordered Zulu into a panic, to turn a retreat into a rout, and to transform a victory into a decisive triumph for the British.

That an exultant pursuit was the ugliest face of colonial war was clearly revealed at Ulundi. There is unfortunately no doubt that the British revelled in it. As the Military Secretary at Fort Pearson telegraphed: 'Cavalry slipped at them (the Zulu). Lancers cut fugitives into mincemeat.' An NCO of the Lancers wrote home to his brother callously commenting that such a 'glorious go-in' made up for all the discomforts he had suffered on campaign, and that 'pig-sticking was fool to it'. The night after the battle the Lancers proudly showed off their lance-pennons, all caked with blood, and negligently passed off their deadly work as being 'just like tent-pegging at Aldershot'. Several officers were loud in their boasts that they had killed four Zulu each.

Yet for all its savagery, the cavalry's counter-attack was a complete success in achieving its objectives. At 9.25 am, after hesitating for a few minutes

The charge of the 17th Lancers at Ulundi. (*The Graphic*, 20 September 1879.)

to give the order until the Zulu retreat was general, Lord Chelmsford directed Colonel Drury-Lowe to pursue the Zulu, and raised his helmet to the men. Five troops of the 17th Lancers (one troop remained inside the square unbeknown to their commander), and 24 men of the King's Dragoon Guards under Captain Brewster, filed out of the square from right of the 94th and left of the 21st. They formed up to the rear of the square, where they were met by a heavy fire from a large body of Zulu who had remained hidden in the long grass. Their firing, though, was ineffective, and the cavalry ignored them, charging initially in the direction of kwaNodwengu to the cheers of the infantry and shouting their war-cry of 'Death! Death!' The Lancers, having soon dispersed or killed those Zulu who had been unable to reach the shelter of kwaNodwengu, and discovering that there were too few Zulu in its vicinity to make their presence worthwhile, halted, and then wheeled right-about to confront large numbers of Zulu who were again concentrating to the right-rear of the square. In a furious charge they pursued the Zulu who scattered in an attempt to reach the lower slopes of the hills about 3 km away, overtaking and killing the men who were running away nearly as fast as the horses could gallop. By the the time the Lancers had driven the Zulu to the base of the hills they began to realize that the ground had become too difficult for cavalry. Moreover, the Zulu were now rallying on the hills to receive them and, reinforced by some of the reserves, were firing on the floundering cavalry, whose horses were by this stage 'a good deal pumped'. So recognizing that the pursuit could not be continued, and having no fresh troops in support, the cavalry wisely rallied and retired with some loss out of range of the Zulu.

The Lancers felt they had proved their worth that day, and vindicated the use of the lance which, although as anachronistic as the infantry square, was invaluable against irregular troops scattered in flight. Despite a tendency to stick in the shield it had penetrated, which had persuaded the cavalry to resort temporarily to their heavy sabres, it was quickly recognized that only the lance was effective when the Zulu flung themselves flat or sheltered in crevasses. Although some of the Zulu avoided the deadly thrusts of the lances in this way, many of the pursued desperately turned and fought for their lives in stubborn knots, never crying for quarter. They dodged among the horses, firing at them, stabbing at their bellies and sometimes seizing a lance in an attempt to drag the horseman from his saddle.

Meanwhile, Captain Browne and the Mounted Infantry of the Flying Column moved out of the square in support of the Lancers. They fired into the flank of the Zulu retreating before the cavalry, and eventually merged into their line. The rest of Buller's mounted men dashed out of the right front corner of the

The mounted pursuit. Sketch by Lt. W.F. Fairlie.

square a few minutes after the Lancers began their charge to the accompaniment of the usual cheers. Captain Cochrane and the Natal Native Horse, who were in the lead, chased the Zulu beyond oNdini until they reached the Zulu reserve. The Zulu turned when overtaken by Buller's horsemen, as they had with the Lancers, first firing at them and then using their assegais, or crouching down to hide in the long grass. The irregular cavalry used their carbines pistol-wise, and probably with more deadly effect than the lance of the cavalry. Like the Lancers, they pursued the Zulu as far as the hills. Once on the hillsides, which were inaccessible to the horses, the Zulu began rallying in groups and turned to fire on Buller's men, who retired in their turn.

The most horrific part of the battle was still to come. The British forces turned to flushing out and killing those Zulu who had succeeded in concealing themselves during the pursuit, or who had feigned death, or who had thought the retreat of their comrades only temporary, and had not joined the flight. Yet whatever their reason for lingering on the fatal plain, they also died hard in the end, fighting to the last and never crying out for mercy. Some of Buller's black irregular cavalry, for example, attacked and killed about 70 Zulu who had been cut off in a donga to the rear of the Lancers as they charged. Others thoroughly searched the ground, dispatching Zulu who had taken refuge in other dongas, in long grass, or in the pools and under the banks of the Mbilane stream. The regimental mascot of the 17th Lancers, a great cross-bred dog, distinguished himself in his regiment's eyes by running about and barking furiously whenever he came upon a living Zulu in the grass. The Natal Native Horse in particular were both thorough and cruel, under no circumstances sparing an enemy, even if wounded. Hours after the battle was over the popping of their carbines told of their horrible work, from which they were not to be dissuaded. Yet even then, the wretched Zulu fugitives, if not too badly wounded, would try to sell their lives dearly. The horsemen, even if they took too much delight in their self-appointed task as executioners, had at least played a courageous part in the battle. Not so the Natal Native Contingent who, when all was once again safe, emerged from behind the wagons in the middle of the laager to kill disabled Zulu and plunder the *amakhanda*. As a consequence of this activity, only two Zulu prisoners were taken alive that day.

This aspect of the day's work was hardly one of which the British could be proud, or of which they were inclined to boast. Major Robinson could only beg his correspondent, to whom he had confessed witnessing the assegaing of the Zulu wounded, not to mention it to others 'or they will think us awful brutes, as bad as we did the Bashi-bazouks'.

As the main body of Zulu retreated in great masses over the hills to the north, all the 9-pounder guns were moved up to shell them. They opened fire at 9.40 am on the Zulu who were squatting down in exhausted groups on the hilltops, especially the hills 4 800 m away to the north, and in a kloof near oNdini. The shrapnel bursts rapidly caused the Zulu resting on the hills to scatter, and after a few rounds they had disappeared from the sight of the British. The Zulu told how the shells fired after them did little damage as they burst too high, though it does seem that what casualties they suffered were mainly women, who had been watching the battle from what they had thought to be the security of the hills.

While the Zulu vanished from the hills the British officers crowded around to congratulate Chelmsford, and the soldiers cheered their generals. The British dead were buried in their uniforms where they had fallen, and a clergyman read the burial service over them as the men stood bare-headed. Once the wounded had been attended to and were fit to be removed on stretchers, then at 11.30 am the troops, still in their square formation, moved down to the banks of the Mbilane stream. There the men rested and had their dinner. Meanwhile, the mounted men continued to scour the surrounding plain, where within an hour of the beginning of the pursuit there was not a Zulu remaining except wounded or dead.

Beside flushing out Zulu fugitives, the British mounted units were engaged in setting all the *amakhanda* in the plain ablaze, or in completing their destruction. Among those burned were oNdini, kwaNodwengu, kwaBulawayo, kwaKhandempemvu, kwaGqikazi, kwaNdabakawombe, kwaMbonambi and emLambongwenya, as well as more distant ones of less importance. At 10.07 am the 9-pounders shelled oNdini and drove out over the hills a large concentration of Zulu who were still sheltering there. It was then that Chelmsford ordered the cavalry and the irregular horsemen, who had returned to the shelter of the square for a short rest after their pursuit, to go out once more and burn oNdini. So began a race between the mounted officers for the honour of being the first at Cetshwayo's 'capital'. Lord William Beresford narrowly beat Commandant Baker to their goal. It was lucky for these single horsemen that in this and the other *amakhanda* they encountered no resistance, though the body of the Hon. W. Drummond, Chelmsford's intelligence officer, was later found in the charred ruins of oNdini. It would seem that he had lost his way among the huts, and that some of the few Zulu still seen there had killed him.

Buller ordered the firing of oNdini at 11.40 am while the infantry relaxed by the Mbilane. His men moved from hut to hut with flaming torches of grass. It seems, though, that the Zulu themselves, having stripped the *ikhanda* bare, had first set fire to it, though for lack of wind the huts did not burn freely and the British effectively completed the work. There is evidence that the Zulu started the firing of the neighbouring *amakhanda* as well. That they did so is not the least extraordinary, especially considering the precedent of their burning of emGungundlovu, King Dingane's *ikhanda*, which he had ordered after the defeat of Blood River in 1838. In any event, oNdini made an enormous bonfire, which smouldered for four days. It might have been a 'grand sight' for the victors to see all the *amakhanda* of the plain sending up their columns of smoke,

National Army Museum, Chelsea.

View from the British camp on the White Mfolozi of the burning of oNdini and other *amakhanda* in the Mahlabathini plain.

but for the Zulu, looking down from the surrounding peaks, or those further afield seeing the thick haze of smoke covering the country, it was a clear sign that their kingdom had fallen. It signified the same to Captain Slade, watering his horses in the Mbilane. He voiced the general British sentiment when he wrote to his mother that 'we all felt at last that the power of the Zulus had been destroyed'.

Chapter Five
ASSESSING THE COST

Lord Chelmsford and General Newdigate addressed their men while they were by the Mbilane stream watching the flames engulf oNdini. They praised their conduct in the battle and especially their steadiness at firing, which had been indeed the crucial factor. At about 2 pm, after a good rest, the British began their return march to their camp at the White Mfolozi, reaching it in stages between 3.30 and 5.30 pm. The band of the 1/13th, which was the only military band present at the battle with its instruments, played the troops back with 'Rule Britannia', 'God Save the Queen' and the 'Royal Alliance March'. The step was given by their old drum, captured from the Afghans in 1849. The pace of march was very slow because of the wounded who had to be carried on stretchers.

Africana Museum, Johannesburg.

The band of the 1/13th Light Infantry in Zululand.

A Zulu shield taken from kwaNodwengu and presented to Queen Victoria. It still hangs — with some other items — as a trophy at Osborne House, once Queen Victoria's residence on the Isle of Wight.

In all, the British had lost 2 officers and 10 men killed, 1 officer wounded (who died on 14 July), and 69 men wounded. An indication of their wounds was given by Lord St Vincent's description of those suffered by the 17th Lancers: assegai wounds in chest, back or leg; grazes and torn coats; perforated helmets, water-bottles and saddles. The only fatality and all the serious wounds were from bullets. Horses suffered badly in the battle, 28 being killed and 45 wounded.

The leisurely pace of the British withdrawal to their camp can also be ascribed to the burden of looted shields and assegais carried by the men. Everyone was determined to carry away some memento of the battle, especially a Zulu weapon. The assegai, for example, which Lord William Beresford took from the Zulu he killed on the reconnaissance of 3 July, was destined for a corner of his mother's drawing-room. Yet the 'disadvantage' of such spoils was that they could not readily be worn by the soldiers' womenfolk, and the dearth of other, more decorative 'curiosities' was deplored. The only items of monetary value found in the plain were the three tusks of ivory discovered in Cetshwayo's European-style house which was burnt with the rest of oNdini. These fell to Lord William Beresford, Commandant Baker and Captain Cochrane.

That night the victorious British enjoyed their ration of rum, congratulated each other and compared their wounds. All triumphantly agreed that the Zulu challenge to fight them in the open rather than from behind the protection of their laager had been 'fairly answered'. Certainly, that was the view of Lord Chelmsford, who felt that by proving that they were capable of victory in the open field, British arms had been vindicated throughout southern Africa.

As for the Zulu, it was for them to suffer the bitterness of defeat. Their dead lay in the plain that night, for the British did not trouble to bury any of the Zulu they had killed. Those who had been hit by shell or rocket fire were terribly mutilated, while those killed by Martini bullets were only relatively disfigured.

How many Zulu had died? The official British estimation of Zulu losses was set at 'not less than 1 500', though exaggerated estimates reached 2 500. When on 9 August a British patrol went over the ground, they found no more than 300 skeletons. But this indicated not that the Zulu had suffered few casualties, but that the Zulu had been able to dispose of many of their dead, and had carried away their weapons. Furthermore, in the early stages of the battle the Zulu had been able to evacuate many of their casualties. Yet the great problem in trying to reach any accurate assessment of Zulu losses is the fact that the dead lay in twos and threes for kilometres around, on plain and hilltop, having been killed by shell, rocket, lance or rifle. Naturally, most of the casualties were concentrated within a 400 m radius of the square, where the fight had been its hottest. Norris-Newman considered that on 4 July the British left between 5 and 600 Zulu lying dead within the range of the rifles in the square. Buller himself estimated that his irregular cavalry had inflicted a loss of at least 450 in pursuit. And if Captain Shepstone put the figure at nearer 300, he nevertheless admitted that the pursuit had 'become Butchery rather at last'. The regular cavalry took credit for 150 'kills'. In all, therefore, it seems that the figure of 1 500 (or a 10 per cent casualty rate) is reasonable, especially when it is taken into account that most of the wounded would never have survived, even if they managed to reach their homes.

The Zulu army itself speedily dispersed all over the country after its defeat, and the British, wherever they were in Zululand, noticed returning warriors crossing their lines of communication in considerable numbers. For a while the bush in the country to the north and east of oNdini was clogged with old men, women, girls, children and cattle fleeing from the plain, as well as wounded men from the battle.

King Cetshwayo himself was one of this number. When the look-outs he had posted reported that his army was defeated he immediately retired north-east from kwaMbonambi, crossing the neck of the Ntabenkulu range into the bush beyond, where he was later joined by Mnyamana and tne other important chiefs. Warriors of the uMcijo *ibutho* followed the king some distance as he fled,

A photograph of the Mahlabathini plain nine months after the battle of Ulundi.

but he soon sent them back as he feared their presence would attract attention and alert the enemy to his whereabouts. The king travelled on foot with the women of his *isigodlo* and a number of servants. Weighed down with calamity, he spoke hardly a word. The following day he sent his household and cattle to seek sanctuary with Chief Zibhebhu in the north-eastern reaches of Zululand, and himself moved on to Mnyamana's ekuShumayeleni homestead, which he reached the third day after the battle. There he stayed for a month, attempting fruitlessly to negotiate with the British.

On the morning of 5 July his conquerors stood to arms at 5 am in their camp at the White Mfolozi, and by 7 am were on their way back to their bivouac of 30 June below the Mthonjaneni heights. In the plain they left behind them there was not a sign of life, only the unburied Zulu dead and the smouldering *amakhanda*. The British reached their bivouac only by 2.30 pm, for their progress had been much slowed down because of having to carry the wounded. The Second Division, however, pressed on to reach the laager on the Mthonjaneni heights that evening, and were joined there the next day (6 July) by the Flying Column. A storm of bitterly cold wind, rain and hail began that night, and made all further movement impossible until 9 July. On that day the Flying Column began its march back to KwaMagwaza and St Paul's to link up with Crealock's First Division; while on 10 July the Second Division began to retrace the steps of its earlier advance, and moved back on Fort Evelyn.

Chelmsford's critics seized on this withdrawal which, they contended, by not following up the advantage gained by the victory of Ulundi, unnecessarily prolonged the war. Yet if the shortage of supplies, the encumbrance of the wounded, and the need to get his men under better cover made the move desirable to Chelmsford, what made it possible and realistic was his knowledge that the Zulu army had dispersed following its defeat. It was simply not possible for the Zulu to strike another blow against the invaders until such time as it reassembled. This was a truth recognized even by Chelmsford's highly critical replacement, Sir Garnet Wolseley. And like many another serving officer, Wolseley was very aware that the Zulu army was highly unlikely to answer any fresh call to come together again. And it would not do so because Chelmsford's victory was indeed a decisive one, whatever some modern historians may contend. After his defeat at Blood River in 1838, King Dingane had set out with his army to beyond the Black Mfolozi, where near the Vuna River it re-established his emGundundlovu *ikhanda*. It was very different after Ulundi. King Cetshwayo wished to reassemble the iNgobamakhosi, uMcijo, uMbonambi and uNokhenke *amabutho* to build a new *ikhanda* for him north of the Black Mfolozi. But they ignored his orders and stayed at home. They did so because in the eyes of the Zulu people the war was now over and the king's power gone, and it was pointless to drag out a hopeless struggle.

Indeed, the effects of the battle of Ulundi were immediately apparent. General Wood noted that from the moment the battle had been won, Wood's Irregulars (black auxiliaries recruited in Zululand) were willing to travel anywhere in the country with a message, as they no longer feared to be attacked. The Zulu everywhere openly acknowledged to the British that their defeat was complete and that the war was over. They were generally confounded at being defeated in the open, and felt that the king's prestige was fatally damaged. In fact, the predominant Zulu attitude was that they had had enough of war, that they wanted peace and to be able to go home to resume the normal course of their lives. Everywhere was the hope that the British, having made their point, would go home too.

With the Zulu returning to their homesteads and declaring they would fight no more, Wolseley was able to complete his pacification of Zululand and to capture the king with drastically reduced forces. As organized resistance by the royal armies was over, there remained only a few minor skirmishes still to be fought in the remote north-western corner of Zululand. Otherwise, not a further blow was struck. In the weeks following, the chiefs steadily negotiated terms with the British, or made their submissions. On 1 September they formally accepted the terms of Wolseley's settlement, which abolished the kingdom and divided it into thirteen fragments to be ruled by nominated chiefs. The British had at last gained their objective of destroying the power of the Zulu state. To achieve this, it had been necessary to break the might of the Zulu army, and with it the authority of the king. The battle of Ulundi had effected both.

Chronology

11 December 1878 presentation of British ultimatum to Zulu king

11 January 1879 first British invasion of Zululand begins

22 January Right Column fights through Zulu ambush at Nyezane

22 January Zulu army overwhelms camp of British Centre Column at Isandlwana

22-23 January British garrison at Rorke's Drift holds off attack by part of Zulu army

23 January Centre Column retires to Natal

28 January Right Column decides to hold fast at Fort Eshowe, where Zulu blockade it

31 January Left Column entrenches at Khambula hill, and raids surrounding countryside

12 March Zulu destroy British convoy and escort at Ntombe river

28 March Chelmsford leads Eshowe Relief Column into Zululand

28 March Zulu rout British patrol from Khambula on Hlobane mountain

29 March Left Column routs main Zulu army at Khambula

2 April Eshowe Relief Column routs Zulu army at Gingindlovu

3 April Eshowe garrison relieved and evacuated to Natal

21 April second invasin begins with building of supply depots up Zulu coast for First Division

June Zulu army musters at oNdini

1 June Second Division advances across Blood River into Zululand

17 June Second Division and Flying Column (reorganized Left Column) join up for march on oNdini under Lord Chelmsford

19 June First Division advances across Thukela River into Zululand

26 June Chelmsford's men burn *amakhanda* at emaKhosini

27 June Chelmsford encamps on Mthonjaneni heights

28 June First Division encamps at Port Durnford in Mlalazi plain

30 June Chelmsford encamps at foot of Mthonjaneni

1 July Chelmsford encamps at White Mfolozi

2 July Chelmsford fortifies camp at White Mfolozi

2 July King Cetshwayo's last attempt to negotiate

3 July Zulu ambush Buller's patrol reconnoitring Mahlabathini plain

2–4 July Sir Garnet Wolseley unable to land at Port Durnford

4 July battle of Ulundi and flight of King Cetshwayo

19 July surrender of coastal chiefs to Wolseley

15 August surrender of principal chiefs to Wolseley near oNdini

28 August capture of King Cetshwayo

1 September chiefs accept Wolseley's terms for a settlement

2 September British begin evacuation of Zululand

Glossary of military terms

abattis: defences made of felled trees and bushes
aide-de-camp: officer assisting his commander by carrying orders, etc.
artillery: large guns mounted on wheels for transport; or the branch of the army using these
auxiliaries: temporary soldiers raised to help regular troops
bayonet: stabbing blade attachable to rifle
bivouac: temporary encampment without tents
breastwork: a hastily constructed defensive earthwork about a metre high
cadet: student in military skills
carbine: short barrelled rifle for cavalry use
case-shot: bullets in a container which spray out when fired from a gun
cavalry: soldiers mounted on horses
deploy: to spread out and place troops
detachments: portions of an armed force employed separately
details: small bodies of soldiers set apart for special duties
dress ranks: to straighten ranks of soldiers and set them in proper order
echelon: a stepwise arrangement in parallel parts, each with its front clear of the part in front
entrenching-tools: short-handled spades, etc. carried by soldiers for digging trenches and throwing up earthworks
facings: cuffs, collar etc. of a soldier's tunic coloured differently from the rest
flank: right or left side of a body of troops
garrison: troops stationed to defend a fort, etc.
grape-shot: small balls in a container which spray out when fired from a gun
half-open order: military formation with quite wide spaces between the men
infantry: soldiers who fight on foot
irregular cavalry: part-time, voluntary mounted soldiers, raised in time of emergency, not highly disciplined and sometimes using unconventional and flexible fighting methods
kit: a soldier's personal equipment packed for travelling
laager: a defensive formation of parked wagons surrounded by a trench
muster: assembling of soldiers
outflank: to pass around, or overlap the side or wing of an opposing body of soldiers

patrol: detachment of troops sent out to learn position and condition of the enemy
picquets: small bodies of troops sent out to watch for the enemy
pig-sticking: the hunting with a spear on horseback of wild boar
range marker: a marker set up outside a defensive position to help the defenders sight their weapons accurately when attacked
regular cavalry: full-time, professional mounted soldiers, highly disciplined and conventional in fighting methods
reveille: bugle and drum call sounded in the morning to awaken soldiers
shrapnel: shower of metal splinters from an exploding shell
skirmishing order: very loose military formation with wide spaces between the men
sortie: sudden rush of defenders against those attacking them
square: a tight formation of infantry, several ranks deep, designed to fight off a cavalry charge, the empty space in the middle being filled with reserves, ammunition-carts, ambulances, etc.
supports: troops stationed in reserve
tent-pegging: cavalry exercise in which the rider tries to carry off a peg in the ground on the point of his lance while at the gallop
van: the front of an army on the march or in line of battle
volley: simultaneous firing of weapons

References

Given below are specific references to the sources used in the writing of this work.

Private Papers

Hotham Papers (The Brynmore Jones Library, University of Hull)
DDHO/13/18:   H.E. Hotham to his Pater, 5 July 1879
   Hotham to Ella, 7 July 1879

Wolseley Papers (Hove Central Library)
2:   Sir Garnet Wolseley to his Wife, 10 July

Anstruther Papers (National Army Museum, Chelsea)
5707-22:   Col. P. Anstruther's Letter-Book, 4 July

Chelmsford Papers (National Army Museum, Chelsea)
6807-386-9, no. 52:   Wood to Military Secretary, 10 May 1879
6807-386-13, no. 40:   Notes by Drummond on Cetshwayo's peace messages, 5 June 1879
6807-386-13, no. 46:   Crealock to Chelmsford, telegram received 10 June 1879
6807-386-16, no. 14:   Statement of Zulu employed by Wood, 12 May 1879
6807-386-16, no. 35:   Crealock to Chelmsford, 8 June 1879: statement of Umsutu

MacSwiney Papers (National Army Museum, Chelsea)
640-16-2:   Capt. J. MacSwiney to his Mother, 6 July 1879

Roe Papers (National Army Museum, Chelsea)
7508-14:   Cpl. W. Roe's Diary, pp. 65-73

Slade Papers (National Army Museum, Chelsea)
6807-235:   Capt. F. Slade's Diary, 4 July 1879
Slade to his Mother, 6 July 1879

Milne Papers (National Maritime Museum, Greenwich)
MLN 202/2:   Sir A. Milne's Naval Diary, 29 May 1879

Wolseley Papers (Public Record Office, Kew)
WO 147/7:   Sir Garnet Wolseley's South African Journal, 21, 24, 26 June 1879

Woodgate Papers (Collection of Dr G. Kemble Woodgate, Oxford)
Capt. E. Woodgate's Official Military Diary, 7 July 1879
Woodgate's Private Diary, 19 June 1879

Stabb Papers (Johannesburg Public Library)
Col. H. Stabb's Zulu War Diary, 4 July 1879

Alison Collection (The Brenthurst Library, Parktown)
Book no. 6399, Collection of Letters to Sir Archibald Alison:
p. 41, Clery no. 17:   Clery to Alison, 8 July 1879
p. 43, Clery no. 18:   Clery to Alison, 29 June 1879
p. 94, Crealock no. 26:   J. Crealock to Alison, 29 June 1879
p. 97, Crealock no. 27:   J. Crealock to Alison, 2 July 1879
p. 101, nn.:   J. Crealock to Alison, 11 July 1879
p. 127, Russell no. 2:   Russell to Alison, 6 July 1879
p. 141, nn.:   Robinson to Maudie Lefroy, 6 July 1879
p. 143, nn.:   Robinson to Alison, 8 July 1879

Harness Letters (The Brenthurst Library, Parktown)
Book no. 6405, Lt. Col. Arthur Harness to his Sisters:
Harness to Co., July 1879

St. Vincent Journal (The Brenthurst Library, Parktown)
Book no. 6609, Journal of the Fourth Viscount St Vincent:
1, 3, 4-10 July 1879

Colenso Papers (Killie Campbell Africana Library, Durban)
File no. 27, no. 224:   Colenso to Chesson, 25 July 1879

Commeline Letters (Killie Campbell Africana Library, Durban)
D1233/45:   Commeline to his Pater, 18 July 1879

James Stuart Collection (Killie Campbell Africana Library, Durban)
File no. 84:   Ms translation by E.R. Dahle of Stuart, *uKulumetule*, Chap. IV, p. 11

Carle Faye Papers (Natal Archives Depot, Pietermaritzburg)
Box no. 7:   'How We Captured Cetywayo' told by Martin Oftebro

John Shepstone Papers (Natal Archive Depot, Pietermaritzburg)
Vol. 10:   'Reminiscences of the Past', part II

Sir Theophilus Shepstone Papers (Natal Archives Depot, Pietermaritzburg)
Box 41:   Offy to William Shepstone, 17 July 1879

Unpublished Official Papers

War Office Papers (Public Record Office, Kew):
WO 32/7740:   Chelmsford to Secretary of State for War, (?) May 1879
WO 32/7753:   Maj. Gen. Clifford to Secretary of State for War, telegram received 23 July 1879
WO 32/7764:   Wood to Deputy Adjutant-General, 5 July 1879
WO 32/7764:   Glyn to Assistant Adjutant-General, 5 July 1879
WO 32/7764:   Buller to Wood, 5 July 1879
WO 32/7764:   Drury-Lowe to Assistant Adjutant-General, 6 July 1879
WO 32/7767:   Newdigate's Diary, 1, 2, 4 July
WO 33/34:   Chelmsford to Secretary of State for War, 6 July 1879

Colonial Secretary's Office Papers, Natal (Natal Archives Depot, Pietermaritzburg):
CSO 1926, no. 2076:   Fannin to Colonial Secretary, 19 April 1879
CSO 1927, no. 2424:   Fannin to Colonial Secretary, 10 May 1879
CSO 1927, no. 2616:   Fannin to Colonial Secretary, 23 May 1879
CSO 1927, no. 2720:   Fannin to Colonial Secretary, 31 May 1879
CSO 1927, no. 2947:   Fannin to Colonial Secretary, 9 June 1879
CSO 1927, no. 2979:   Fannin to Colonial Secretary, 11 June 1879
CSO 1927, no. 3572:   Fannin to Colonial Secretary, 26 July 1879

Secretary for Native Affairs Papers, Natal (Natal Archives Depot, Pietermaritzburg)
SNA 1/1/33, no. 11:   Fynn to Secretary for Native Affairs, 10 May 1879

Official Printed Sources

British Parliamentary Papers
(C. 2367), sub-enc. 5 in 55:   Wheelwright to Colonial Secretary, 2 May 1879
(C. 2374), enc. 3 in 24:   Fynney to Secretary for Native Affairs, 13 May 1879
(C. 2374), enc. 16 in 32:   Crealock to Frere, 9 June 1879
(C. 2454), enc. in 55:   Chelmsford to O.C. Landman's Drift, telegram, 5 July 1879
   Military Secretary to Captain Parr, telegram, 6 July 1879
(C. 2482), enc. 2 in 23:   Chelmsford to Wolseley, telegram, 6 July 1879
(C. 2482), enc. in 32:   Chelmsford to Secretary of State for War, 6 July 1879
(C. 2482), enc. in 51:   Fannin to Colonial Secretary, (?) June 1879
(C. 2482), 47:   Wood to Deputy Adjutant-General, 27 June 1879
   Chelmsford to Secretary of State for War, 28 June 1879

Callwell, Col. C.E., *Small Wars. Their Principles and Practice* (London, 3rd edit., 1906), pp. 72, 172-4, 190, 201-11, 227-32, 256-71, 378, 386-96, 414-5, 430, 453-6, 440-1

Intelligence Branch of the War Office, *Narrative of the Field Operations Connected with the Zulu War of 1879* (London, 1881), pp. 110-7, 122, 124, 165-5

Newspapers and Periodicals

The Graphic, 16, 30 August, 13 September 1879
The Illustrated London News, 3, 26 July, 23 August, 6 September 1879
The Natal Colonist, 5 July, 20 September 1879
The Natal Mercury, 11, 16 July, 14 August 1879
The Natal Witness, 15, 17 July, 21 August 1879

Contemporary Articles

Forbes, Archibald, 'The Bravest Deed I Ever Saw. How Lord William Beresford Won the VC', *Pearson's Magazine*, 1 (January 1896)
Fripp, C.E., 'Reminiscences of the Zulu War, 1879', *Pall Mall Magazine*, 20 (1900), pp. 556-62
Hutton, Lt.-Gen. Sir E., 'Some Recollections of the Zulu War', *The Army Quarterly*, XVI (April 1921), pp. 79-80
Colley, Sir George Pomeroy, 'Army', *Encyclopaedia Britannica*, 9th edition, vol. II (Edinburgh, 1875), pp. 572-80

Contemporary Histories, Reminiscences, and Edited Collections

Ashe, Major & Wyatt Edgell, Capt the Hon. E.V., *The Story of the Zulu Campaign* (London, 1880), pp. 337-54
Colenso, Frances assisted by Durnford, Lieut.-Col. E., *History of the Zulu War and its Origin* (London, 1880), pp. 440-52
Dawnay, G.C., *Private Journal of Guy C. Dawnay* (private circulation), pp. 66-70
Harrison, Gen. Sir R. *Recollections of a Life in the British Army* (London, 1908), pp. 182-7

Malet, Capt T. St Lo., *Extracts from a Diary in Zululand* (Upper Norwood, 1880), pp. 23-30
McToy, E.D., *A Brief History of the 13th Regiment (P.A.L.I.) in South Africa during the Transvaal and Zulu Difficulties* (Devonport, 1880), pp. 76-95
Mitford, Bertram, *Through the Zulu Country* (London, 1883), pp. 161, 229-38
Molyneux, Maj.-Gen. W.C.F., *Campaigning in South Africa and Egypt* (London, 1896), pp. 177-90
Molyneux, Major W.C.F., *Notes on Hasty Defences as Practised in South Africa* (private circulation, 1879), p. 3
Montague, Capt W.E., *Campaigning in South Africa. Reminiscences of an Officer in 1879* (Edinburgh & London, 1880), pp. 226-36, 280-1, 310-11
Moodie, D.C.F. (ed.), *The History of the Battles and Adventures of the British, the Boers and the Zulus in Southern Africa* (Sidney, Melbourne and Adelaide, 1879), pp. 352-68, 442
Mossop, George, *Running the Gauntlet* (London, 1937), pp. 76-96
Norris-Newman, C.L., *In Zululand with the British throughout the War of 1879* (London, 1880), pp. 206-16, 235-6, 318-26
Plé, James, *Les Laagers dans la Guerre des Zoulous* (Paris, 1882), pp. 14-5
Prior, Melton, *Campaigns of a War Correspondent* (London, 1912), pp. 118-9
Tomasson, W.H., *With the Irregulars in the Transvaal and Zululand* (London, 1881), pp. 140-208
Vijn, Cornelius (tr. and ed. Bishop Colenso), *Cetshwayo's Dutchman* (London, 1880), pp. 45-53, 142-4
Wood, Field Marshal Sir Evelyn, *From Midshipman to Field Marshal* (London, 1906), vol. II, pp. 79-81
Wood, W. (ed.), *Marvellous Escapes from Peril as Told by Survivors* (London, Glasgow, Bombay, 19-(?), pp. 23-32

Later Edited Collections of Contemporary Sources

Dlamini, Paulina (comp. H. Filter, ed. & tr. S. Bourquin), *Servant of Two Kings* (Durban & Pietermaritzburg), pp. 29, 70-1, 116
Emery, Frank (ed.), *The Red Soldier. Letters from the Zulu War, 1879* (London, 1977), pp. 224-38
Emery, Frank (ed.), 'At War with the Zulus 1879. The Letters of Lieut. C.E. Commeline, RE', *Royal Engineers Journal*, 96, 1 (March 1982), pp. 37-8
Fuze, Magema M. (tr. H.C. Lugg & ed. A.T. Cope), *The Black People and Whence They Came. A Zulu View* (Pietermaritzburg & Durban, 1979), pp. 114-5
Webb, C. de B. & Wright, J.B. (eds.), *A Zulu King Speaks* (Pietermaritzburg & Durban, 1978), pp. 34-5, 58-9
Webb, C. de B. & Wright, J.B. (eds. & trs.), *The James Stuart Archive of Recorded Oral Evidence* (Pietermaritzburg & Durban, 1986), vol. IV, pp. 72-3, 280-1, 288, 373

Later Articles, Books, Pamphlets, Reports and Theses

Binns, C.T., *The Last Zulu King* (London, 1963), pp. 157-166
Chadwick, G.A., *The Zulu War of 1879. The Second Invasion of Zululand and the Battle of Ulundi* (pamphlet, n.d.)
Chadwick, G.A., *Research on Historical Places of Importance to KwaZulu and the Formulation of Recommendations* (unpublished, 1983), pp. C17A-C21
Clarke, Sonia, 'Ulundi: Two Views of the Battle', in Ian Knight (ed.), *There will be an Awful Row at Home about This* (Shoreham-by-Sea, 1987), pp. 32-3
Featherstone, D., *Weapons & Equipment of the Victorian Soldier* (Poole, 1978), pp. 26-30, 34-8, 53-65, 85-99, 119
Gibson, J.Y., *The Story of the Zulus* (London, 1911), pp. 212-3
Guy, Jeff, *The Destruction of the Zulu Kingdom* (Great Britain, 1979), pp. 54-9
Guy, Jeff, 'The British Invasion of Zululand', *Reality*, 11, 1 (January 1979), pp. 12-14

Hall, Major D.D., 'Artillery in the Zulu War', *Military History Journal*, 4, 4 (January 1979), pp. 155-61

Laband, J.P.C. & Thompson, P.S., *Field Guide to the War in Zululand and the Defence of Natal 1879* (Pietermaritzburg, 1983), pp. 3-11, 22-3, 94-5

Laband, J.P.C., 'The Zulu Army in the War of 1879', *Journal of Natal and Zulu History*, II (1979), pp. 27-35

Laband, J.P.C., 'The Cohesion of the Zulu Polity under the Impact of the Anglo-Zulu War', *Journal of Natal and Zulu History*, VIII (1985), pp. 46-62

Laband, J.P.C., 'Humbugging the General? King Cetshwayo's Peace Overtures during the Anglo-Zulu War', *Theoria*, 67 (October 1986), pp. 1-20

Langley, D.E., 'The Organisation of the British Army', in Ian Knight (ed.), *There will be an Awful Row at Home about This* (Shoreham-by-Sea, 1987), pp. 34-6

Lugg, H.C., *Historic Natal and Zululand* (Pietermaritzburg, 1949), pp. 112-4, 142-4

Mathews, J., 'Lord Chelmsford: British General in Southern Africa 1878-9', (unpublished D. Litt. et Phil. thesis, UNISA, 1987), pp. 292-339

Morris, D.R., *The Washing of the Spears* (London, 1966), pp. 556-575

Wilkinson-Latham, C., *Uniforms & Weapons of the Zulu War* (Manchester, 1978), pp. 16-70